The 4P's of You

Expanded Edition

Purpose, Passion, Persistence, Planning
Trunnis Goggins II
Foreword by Sam Humphrey

© 2025 Trunnis Goggins II

Book Cover Design: Nichol Perricci

Interior Book Design & Formatting: DNP Presents

ALL RIGHTS RESERVED. No part of this book may be reproduced in any written, electronic, recording, or photocopying without written permission of the publisher or author. The exception would be in the case of brief quotations embodied in critical articles or reviews and pages where permission is specifically granted by the publisher or author.

LEGAL DISCLAIMER. Although the author has made every effort to ensure that the information in this book was correct at press time, the author does not assume hereby disclaim any liability to any party for loss, damage, or disruption caused by errors or omissions, whether such errors or omissions result from negligence, accident, or any other cause.

Published By: DNP Presents

Library of Congress Cataloging-in-Publication Data has been applied for

ISBN: 979-8-9988576-6-9

PRINTED IN THE UNITED STATES OF AMERICA

Table of Contents

Foreword by Sam Humphrey .... page 7

Chapter 1 .... page 23
    Embracing the Journey: The Story Behind the Expanded Edition

Chapter 2 .... page 27
    Progress is Not Always Forward

Chapter 3 .... page 39
    Your Role in the Lives of Others

Chapter 4 .... page 51
    What Do You Want?

Chapter 5 .... page 63
    The Evolution of Purpose

Chapter 6 .... page 69
    You Can't Force Purpose

Chapter 7 .... page 73
    It's All in the Planning

Chapter 8 .... page 83
    Positive Planning

Chapter 9 .... page 95
    Planning with the Strategic Mindset

Chapter 10 .... page 117
    The Right Team to Execute Your Game Plan

Chapter 11 .... page 125
    Passion

Chapter 12 .... page 136
Passion and People

Chapter 13 .... page 150
Persistence

Chapter 14 .... page 163
The Contingency Plan

Chapter 15 .... page 177
There Will Be Pain Regardless

Chapter 16 .... page 182
Time to Relax

Chapter 17 .... page 189
The Power of Trying Something New

I couldn't do it without YOU!

Foreword
Sam Humphrey

Let me start by saying how grateful I am to know and be friends with Trunnis Goggins. He is a wise, thoughtful, passionate, hardworking, supportive, kind, and always-on-the-move type of person. I have the deepest and utmost respect for him and everything he's done.

Simply put, I think he's a badass.

It's a deep honor and a privilege to be considered—let alone asked—to write the foreword for this book, *The 4P's of You*.

Not only am I proud to call him a friend, but I also have the pleasure of working with him on this project, another anthology called *The NEXT Best You*, and some upcoming joint talks on stage.

This is more than a book. It's a guide to how you can discover Purpose, Planning, Passion, and Persistence within yourself.

Why me? Why this book?

I believe Trunnis asked me to write this because of the life experience I've lived—not because I have it all figured out, because believe me, I don't. Through my journey to becoming the man I am today, I've discovered what the 4P's truly mean—and how they shape not just what I do, but why I do it.

In the end, everything we build in life comes down to our why: your career, your relationships, your faith, your friendships. You might have smaller whys for different seasons, but the big WHY—the one that grounds you—matters most.

Today, we live in a world of constant distraction, comparison, and burnout. Everything is so readily accessible that if we can't have something quickly, we're tempted to give up. It's no wonder so many people—even those who seem successful—wrestle with a deep sense of unfulfillment.

We learn to survive, to perform, to stay busy, convincing ourselves that it's enough, even when something deeper inside us knows it's not.

At some point, most of us wake up with the uncomfortable realization that we're living on autopilot. And here's the truth: you don't get to choose where you're born, who your family is, or whether you get hurt. Life will test you—whether through your own choices or by the hand you're dealt.

But you always get to choose how you respond.

THE 4P'S OF YOU

Purpose. Planning. Passion. Persistence.

These aren't just ideas. They are foundations you can build your life on if you want to accomplish anything truly meaningful.

And I can tell you from experience: I know what it's like to feel like you're living on autopilot, adrift on the sea of life, going nowhere fast.

Let me share with you when I discovered and harnessed the power of the 4P's—and how they continue to shape my journey. Because no matter where you're starting, or what season you're in, these principles can help you find your way too.

I am a little person, and at the time of writing this, I'm turning 31 years old. Maybe you know me from my role as Tom Thumb in *The Greatest Showman*, a film that, at that point, marked one of the biggest milestones of my acting career.

But it wasn't an easy road to get there. I have faced emotional, mental, and physical battles, especially after being diagnosed with Crohn's Disease. It's a journey of setbacks, of resilience, and of constant rediscovery.

I'm still a work in progress. Still figuring this thing called *LIFE* out, one day at a time.

One of my favorite quotes—one that has stuck with me since I first heard it—is from *Rocky Balboa*, spoken by Sylvester Stallone:

> *"Let me tell you something you already know. The world ain't all sunshine and rainbows. It's a very mean and nasty place, and I don't care how tough you are, it will beat you to your knees and keep you there permanently if you let it. You, me, or nobody is gonna hit as hard as life. But it ain't about how hard you hit. It's about how hard you can get hit and keep moving forward; how much you can take and keep moving forward. That's how winning is done!"*

> *"Now, if you know what you're worth, then go out and get what you're worth. But you gotta be willing to take the hits, and not pointing fingers saying you ain't where you wanna be because of him, or her, or anybody. Cowards do that and that ain't you. You're better than that!"*

That quote isn't just about toughness. It's about clarity. Ownership. Refusing to blame your circumstances—and choosing to move forward no matter what.

To me, it reflects all four of the principles in this book: Purpose, Planning, Passion, and Persistence.

Life will hit you; that's a given. But if you've done the work to know your why (Purpose), laid the track to move forward (Planning), kept your fire lit (Passion), and refused to quit (Persistence), you'll still be standing—and still moving forward.

That's why understanding the 4P's isn't just helpful; it's necessary.

Each one builds on the other, and it all starts with the foundation: Purpose.

Purpose – Knowing Your Why

What is purpose, really?

To me, it's the why behind everything you do—the reason you show up, even when it's hard. It's what guides your decisions, your focus, and your fire. But figuring out your why isn't always simple. It took me a long time to understand mine. And to be real with you, I still get in my head about it sometimes.

I'm an over-thinker, especially when it comes to things close to my heart. I used to feel like I had to have a perfect answer, like I couldn't move forward until I could explain my purpose in a way that made sense to everyone else. But what I've come to realize is that purpose evolves—and that's not just okay, it's necessary.

When I was younger, I thought my purpose was to become an actor. But if I'm honest, that "why" came from a place of pain. I wanted to prove something to the world. I wanted to show that I could succeed despite being a little person, despite not fitting the mold. I just wanted to be seen, heard, and taken seriously. At the time, that felt like purpose. But looking back now, I can see it was more about validation than true calling.

Later, my why began to shift. Acting became less about proving myself and more about having a platform. I wanted to create a voice for something bigger than me. I wanted to speak to the causes I cared about. I wanted to help people see others like me—and like them—in a different light. That was growth.

And now, after walking through storms I never asked for, my purpose has deepened even more. Today, my why is rooted in service. Through acting, through speaking, and through my brand, The Little Guy Collective, I want to be a voice for those who feel invisible.

I want people to know they are loved, worthy, and valuable—not because of what they do, but because of who they are.

Being broken or different doesn't disqualify you. You don't need to be perfect to have purpose. You just need to be willing.

THE 4P'S OF YOU

Purpose isn't about titles, applause, or achievement. It's about knowing who you are, why you're here, and who you're becoming in the process.

The road to discovering my purpose wasn't easy. I wanted to give up more times than I can count. There were days when I was ready to walk away entirely—from acting, from faith, from life itself. I even tried to. But God wasn't done with me. And He's not done with you either.

Pain shapes purpose. It refines it. Like it says in Romans:

> *"Suffering produces perseverance; perseverance, character; and character, hope."* — Romans 5:3–4

I know what it feels like to question your worth. To battle suicidal thoughts. To live in a world that doesn't seem to have space for you. I know what it's like to live with chronic illness, like Crohn's Disease, and feel like your body is working against you.

But even in those moments—even when it felt like my purpose had disappeared—God never left me. And that's what anchors me now.

You are inherently valuable because you are a beautiful HUMAN BEING made in the image of GOD. He loves you unconditionally. So much so, that He sent His Son, Jesus, to die on a cross—so that we shall be forgiven and fully reconciled to Him when we truly accept what He did for us.

That's what faith is. It's not about perfection. It's about trusting in His love, turning away from what holds us back, and stepping into the freedom He's already made possible.

> "For God so loved the world, that he gave his only begotten Son, that whosoever believeth in him should not perish, but have everlasting life." — John 3:16

That truth gives my purpose meaning. It's the anchor beneath everything else.

But here's the thing: purpose alone isn't enough.

Having a why is powerful, but without a plan, that why can get buried under doubt, distraction, or delay.

And that brings us to the second P: Planning.

Let's talk about how you move from knowing your why to actually living it intentionally—even when life doesn't go according to plan.

Planning – When You Don't Have the Perfect Path, You Map Your Own

That's where planning comes in. A lot of people think planning is about controlling every step, mapping out every detail, and checking every box. But real planning—the kind that actually moves you toward your calling—is about having a vision with flexibility.

I'm a perfectionist and, at times, a bit of a control freak, especially when something reflects back on me. Letting go wasn't easy. But I've learned that holding on too tightly suffocates your plans. It's like a fickle flame that gets snuffed out without enough oxygen. If you don't leave room for flexibility, you might miss the opportunities that were meant for you.

There's a quote I love: *"If you fail to plan, you plan to fail."* And it's true. But what most people don't talk about is what happens when the plan you carefully built goes sideways—because more often than not, it will, especially when you least expect it.

Planning for me wasn't a neat, traditional 1-2-3 formula. Growing up, I spent months in hospitals, missed huge portions of school, and navigated life carrying visible and invisible battles most people never saw. I didn't have the luxury of following a clear, predictable path into the entertainment industry—or into life, really.

All I had was a vision: to become a successful actor.

And while my purpose has evolved over time, that vision has remained. It's just grown wider to fit the calling God's been shaping in me. Planning didn't mean scripting every step perfectly. For me, it meant knowing the bigger picture and staying pointed in that direction—even when life tried to pull me off course.

There were setbacks. Detours. Closed doors. Times when my health knocked me completely out of the race. Seasons where it felt like the dream was slipping away.

If I had clung rigidly to how I thought it was supposed to happen, I would have given up. But because I held tightly to the vision—and stayed flexible about the route—I was able to keep moving forward, even when the map kept changing.

Planning, to me, isn't about scripting your life perfectly. It's about building the kind of faith and resilience that keeps you moving even when life rewrites the script. It's about staying ready—so that when the door cracks open, you don't miss your moment. It's about preparing wisely, working diligently, dreaming boldly—and still being willing to adapt when God redirects your steps.

In all my striving, I kept learning this powerful truth:

> *"A man's heart plans his way, but the Lord directs his steps."* — Proverbs 16:9

So yes, make a plan. Lay out a course for your life. But hold that plan with open hands, because sometimes the greatest stories unfold on roads you didn't even know you were walking.

Still, having a plan isn't enough on its own. Even the best-laid plans can feel empty if something deeper isn't fueling the journey.

So, let's talk about what fuels the journey: Passion.

Passion – The Fire That Fuels the Journey

Purpose gives you, your why. Planning gives you, your how.

But passion... passion is the oxygen that keeps the flame alive, the steady breath that turns a fragile spark into a fire that can endure.

Passion can't be handed to you. Other people can help you discover your purpose. They can even help you build a plan. But no one else can give you the fire to keep going. That part has to come from inside.

That's why passion matters so deeply. Without it, purpose fades. Without it, even the best plans eventually fall apart.

Sometimes passion finds you while you're simply living your life. It changes over time. You can enjoy something without it being the thing you devote your life to. But when you find what you're willing to devote yourself to—I hope it's your passion.

I discovered my love for acting at a young age, and it became my passion; it's all I wanted to do. I loved being in the spotlight because it made me feel like I could be whoever I wanted to be. I needed that—and I was very good at it.

My passion for acting was born out of pain, but it led me toward the purpose I carry today. Acting became the vehicle that helped me step into my identity. It gave me a reason to fight. That passion evolved into something bigger than acting itself. It became about what acting represents: the fuel behind the message.

It's about telling stories that reveal the truth of human connection. It's about pushing boundaries and helping others see that they are loved and seen too. That's what reveals my passion for my work.

I had passion before I discovered my purpose. Before I had a plan. And even now, when I don't have everything figured out, I know if the passion is still burning, I'm on the right path.

Passion isn't about pretending you're never tired or scared. It's about holding onto your why even when the feeling fades. It's about using the gifts God gave you to break through walls—walls built by stereotypes, by fear, by limitation.

It's about remembering that the fire God placed inside your heart isn't meant to be dictated by circumstances. It's meant to outlast them.

> *"Never be lacking in zeal, but keep your spiritual fervor, serving the Lord."* — Romans 12:11

That verse reminds me: passion isn't self-generated. It's fueled by something bigger than you. It's a response to the purpose He's placed inside you and the life He's called you to live.

Purpose gives you the reason. Planning gives you structure. Passion gives you the fire.

But there's one more ingredient—the one that ties it all together when life hits hardest: Persistence.

Because even with purpose, planning, and passion... you will get knocked down.

The real question is: Will you get back up?

Persistence – The Strength to Get Back Up

Purpose gives you the reason. Planning gives you the structure. Passion gives you the fire.

But persistence... persistence is the strength to keep going when everything in you wants to quit.

You can have all the passion in the world, but there will still be days when it feels like nothing is working. Days when the doors stay closed. When your body is tired, your heart is heavy, and the dream feels far away.

That's where persistence steps in. It's the decision to rise one more time than you fall. It's not about perfection. It's about endurance.

Persistence isn't glamorous. It's not flashy or loud. It's built in the unseen moments—when no one is watching, when no one is cheering when there's no guarantee of success.

Persistence is the quiet choice to keep showing up. It's the grit to keeps building even when the foundation feels cracked. It's the refusal to let today's obstacles define tomorrow's outcome.

In my own journey, I've lost count of the setbacks. The auditions I didn't get. The hospital stays that derailed my plans. The seasons when every door seemed slammed shut at once.

If I had measured success only by what I could see in those moments, I would have given up long ago.

But persistence taught me something deeper: growth often happens underground before anyone else can see it. The hardest seasons weren't wasted. They were preparing me. Strengthening me. Stretching my roots deeper for what was coming.

> *"Let us not grow weary in doing good, for at the proper time we will reap a harvest if we do not give up."* — Galatians 6:9

Persistence isn't about pretending everything is easy. It's about trusting that what God planted inside you will bear fruit in His time, not yours. It's about staying faithful when the results don't come overnight.

It's about believing the story He's writing is still unfolding, even when the pages seem blank.

Persistence doesn't guarantee an easy road. It guarantees that you'll finish differently than you started: stronger, wiser, and more anchored in who you were always meant to become.

Because at the end of the day, it's not just about achieving a dream. It's about becoming the person who can carry it—with strength, humility, and grace.

Purpose gives you the reason. Planning gives you the structure. Passion gives you the fire.

But persistence... persistence makes sure you don't lose any of it along the way.

At the end of the day, the 4P's aren't just concepts to understand—they are truths to live by.

Purpose gives you the reason. Planning gives you direction. Passion gives you the fire. And persistence gives you the strength to keep standing when life tries to knock you down.

My hope isn't just that you learn these principles—it's that you *live* them. That you carry them into the battles, the victories, and the quiet moments no one else sees.

Because the life you were made for isn't just waiting for you—it's already inside you, ready to be built one step at a time.

Sam Humphrey

Connect with Sam

IG @thesamhumphrey

CHAPTER 1
Embracing the Journey:
The Story Behind the Expanded Edition

If you are picking up this book for the first time, you may be wondering why a new edition has come so soon after the original release. The answer is simple: I am living what I wrote—and that means never being married to a single plan. Growth requires flexibility. Purpose requires re-evaluation. And to truly serve those I hoped to reach with this book, I knew I needed to make some changes.

When I first released this book through my original publisher, I lacked key knowledge about the publishing process. I did not fully understand the nuances of pricing, distribution, and how to make this book accessible to those who truly needed it. I've since come to recognize that pricing flexibility and reach are critical—so I made the bold decision to change publishers. That risk was not taken lightly. At the time, the book was selling internationally. I was being invited to book fairs, bookstores, and speaking engagements around the world. But I knew there was still a better path ahead.

Yet, through that risk came reward. I've learned so much more about my craft, and I've had the honor of meeting people who embody the very values I wrote about in the original release. One of those individuals is the extraordinary Sam Humphrey, who graciously agreed to write the foreword for this edition. Sam's life is a testimony to the Four Ps: Purpose, Plan, Passion, and Persistence. A native of New Zealand, he left behind everything he knew to pursue a dream of becoming an actor in the United States.

What inspires me about Sam is not just his resume—which includes appearing alongside Hugh Jackman and Zac Efron in one of Disney's highest-grossing films—but the way he moved with purpose, despite immense personal challenges. He crossed hemispheres. He battled health issues. He navigated the complex world of entertainment without entitlement. And yet, he emerged as a giant—not just in talent, but in heart. To me, he's not the 'little man' he sometimes jokingly calls himself. He is a giant in every way that matters.

This expanded edition also provides updates to stories featured in the original version. My dear friend Champ Kelly and my son Zachary Goggins have both continued to evolve in their own Four Ps journeys. Their progress, resilience, and growth deserve to be celebrated. Additionally, I've been moved by the courage and strength of two women whose stories brought me to tears: Tessa Williams and Dr. Angela Bennett. Both have faced unfathomable pain, yet they carry on with radiant smiles and deep commitment to helping others walk a better path.

Their stories—and so many others you'll read in the pages ahead—remind us that there is no such thing as a perfect path to purpose. Your plans will shift. Passion may be tested. And disappointment is all but guaranteed. But it's persistence that will carry you through. And perhaps most importantly, humility. The willingness to admit when something can be done better, and the courage to take action, are what make the difference between stagnation and success.

This new edition is also a reflection of how much I've grown—not just as an author, but as a man, a father, and a speaker. The friends I've made through this book and my podcast are now part of a broader mission. My hope is that this updated version—with its revised stories, new voices, and fresh cover—will serve as a reminder that your purpose is always within reach, even if the route to it changes. Growth is not linear. It is dynamic and often uncomfortable. But it is always worth it.

So, I encourage you not only to read this book, but to share it—with friends, family, colleagues, and organizations that believe in transformation. Let the Four Ps—Purpose, Plan, Passion, and Persistence—serve as your compass. Use the stories within these pages as both inspiration and instruction. And above all, never be afraid to pivot. Change does not mean failure. It often means progress. And progress, after all, is the path to purpose.

Chapter 2

Progress is Not Always Forward

In 2019, I lived in Indianapolis, Indiana. Professionally, three years removed from my PhD, I went from being an associate professor to department chair of business, and on to being a sitting member of the Chancellor's Cabinet in the largest community college system in the United States. Privately, I was married, my children were successful in academics and sports, and I had recently obtained guardianship of my grandson, whose mother (my daughter), had tragically died in the summer of 2015. On the surface, with the exception of the death of my daughter, to those on the outside, I was living the American dream. However, that couldn't be further from the truth. I was miserable.

For about three years, my life consisted of getting up and going to work, going home and sitting on the couch, and waiting to go to work the next day. During this time, the excitement of home life was yardwork and sitting by my outdoor fire pit watching CFL football or a hockey game. Outside of that, I did look forward to my two sons' travel hockey season. It was an opportunity to spend time with them traveling to hockey rinks around the region. However, as far as personal and professional growth, this period of my life was very mundane and stagnant.

Then one day in the summer of 2019, everything came to a head when I had a meeting with my boss. I thought it was going to be a meeting to give an update on how my department was running. The meeting was set up weeks in advance, so I spent time preparing for the meeting with a presentation on the department's current situation and started laying down the groundwork for goals and agendas that I would like to achieve in the upcoming academic year. I was truly looking forward to this meeting, however, that's not what this meeting was for at all.

When I arrived at my boss's office, I was greeted by my boss and the director of human resources. Though I was not in trouble, this meeting was to *"inform"* me that money generated from my department would be spent on windbreakers for staff and personnel. It was my intention to take some of the money and use it to purchase training equipment that can be utilized for students and enhance an academic program. Before I could even give the rationale behind the new equipment, my boss and the HR director had already come to a final decision. In a move that was far away from my character, I simply smiled and stated that it was my pleasure to provide finances for such an item, and I walked out of that meeting feeling like no more than a puppet.

For the rest of that afternoon, I sat in the office and tried to work on reports and training materials. However, more often than not, I found myself reflecting on that meeting and getting more and more angry. I remember leaving work to pick up my son for hockey practice, sitting outside of the rink and asking myself repeatedly - Is this what I worked for?

The incident that I had at work actually caused me to seriously sit back and look at my entire life, both professionally and personally. After three years of going through the motions, I realized I was not on track to obtain what I really wanted out of life. I quickly realized then that I had lost focus, and I even felt that I was not serving a purpose. However, in all actuality, I was serving a purpose. I was just serving the purpose of others and not my purpose. I initially intended to serve. I knew then that that's why I was literally coasting through life like a zombie.

The morning after the incident at work, I decided to take a mental health day. It was summertime, so I decided to go on a very long bike ride. During that ride, I set out to get reacquainted with myself. I thought back to when I originally set out to get my PhD. What I really wanted to do. I wanted to become a full-time professor, work with nonprofits and even start nonprofit organizations with the purpose of instituting and furthering social change. I also wanted to write textbooks and even books similar to the one that I have authored here designed to help the readers gain both education and inspiration to achieve lifelong goals. Once I got reacquainted with those goals and memories, I quickly realized that even though I was a successful college administrator, I was nowhere near the goal that I originally set out to achieve.

Once I realized that I was nowhere where I wanted to be professionally, I then started to reflect on where I was personally. I had gone through great challenges during a four-year time period, and I really had not ever paused to reflect on what was actually happening to me. From June 2015 until August 2019, I had lost my oldest daughter in a tragic homicide, I had changed jobs, I was witness to another child of mine as he began his descent into drug abuse, and had recently gone through quite a lengthy legal battle in order to obtain legal guardianship of my grandson who had just lost his mother. All of these issues put a strain on my entire family and I realized that this was a major contributor to the destruction of my marriage.

I found that I was lost, and the reason I was lost was because I purposely put down my compass. Unfortunately, many are lost for that same reason. We get lost when we constantly lie to ourselves and say that we are okay. We get lost when we try to impress others. We get lost when we try to please others at the expense of our own joy. We get lost when we try to put on a façade that we are able to overcome obstacles without the assistance of others. Any combination of those behaviors will ultimately lead an individual to lose their purpose.

Once I realized that I was going the wrong way, I was aware that I had to make major sacrifices in order to get back on track and once again achieve my original goals and serve my original purpose. Like a mediocre sports team that regains its true desire to win, I had to tear myself down and rebuild almost from the ground up. That meant that I had to leave my comfort zone and venture back to a way of living that I thought I would never have to live again.

Over the next couple weeks, I started making steps to start over and once again set out to achieve the goals that I originally set out to achieve. I reached back into my network of professional contacts to see if there were any jobs as a full-time professor. Full-time professor jobs are extremely hard to come across. In the current academic climate, people who obtain full-time professor jobs usually hold onto them for years and years. In addition, many colleges have opened up the adjunct professorships due to the fact that economically those are more affordable and manageable for college and university budgets. However, in my case I got lucky. I reached out to my prior supervisor at my old university, and she made sure that there was a full-time professor position for me.

This move was humbling due to the fact that I had worked very hard to achieve a position of administrative leadership. However, in order to move forward, I had to step back to the position that I once was so many years ago. As humbling as it was, it was necessary to take this step backward in order to give myself the time and resources necessary to accomplish my goal of writing textbooks, contributing to my academic discipline, and to becoming a coach and mentor in both academia and small business. Though I received a substantial pay cut, I don't remember ever being as satisfied as I was when I was once again accepted to the University in which my academic career began.

Personally, I had to leave the house that I purchased. Though my family continued to live in the house, it was time for me to let go of the hope that that residence was ever going to be my home again. I truly loved that home. I enjoyed working in the yard, and it gave me a sense of accomplishment that I achieved the *"American dream"*. I moved into a two-bedroom apartment about 2 miles from the house so I could stay close to my children. Once again, I was back to going to a laundromat to clean my clothes, and I had to deal with the noisy neighbors who lived above me. This was a type of living that I thought I would never have to experience again.

Despite some of the inconveniences of apartment living, this step was necessary. Through no fault of anyone, my marriage had grown stagnant. We had grown apart and we had nothing to talk about. The misery of our circumstances led to silence, and eventually had a negative effect on the children still at the house. My leaving the house and the subsequent divorce eventually led to a dark cloud being lifted off of the entire family. Though there were some adjustments for everyone, I'm happy to say that the separation allowed everyone to begin to grow again.

With this step back, I rediscovered the joy that I once had for accomplishing goals. Everyone who knew me from that time, my kids included, stated that I seem to be much happier now. That assessment is absolutely correct. Though the step backward did have a major impact on my checking account, I must admit that I am back on track and I'm serving my purpose.

4P's

As a business professor, I am sometimes assigned to teach an introductory marketing class. In that class, my students learn about the 4P's of marketing which are place, price, product, and promotion. All successful marketing campaigns and plans must consider those 4P's. If even one of those "Ps" are missed, marketing could be disastrous.

Something similar can be said about you and me. We have 4P's as well, and our 4P's stand for Purpose, Plan, Passion, and Persistence. And like in marketing, if one of those Ps are not considered, our life can end up in unnecessary turmoil.

Back in 2010, in a Supreme Court ruling on the First Amendment and campaign contributions, the Supreme Court essentially declared corporations and organizations as people. Today, I am unilaterally declaring you a corporation. You have a product and service to sell, you are a brand, and like products and brands you should expect a certain level of loyalty. That loyalty does not necessarily come from others. However, you should demand a certain level of your own loyalty to you.

When deciding what is your true purpose, you must first decide what is your *"product or service"*. In other words, *"What are you good at doing?"* Better yet, *"What are you passionate about doing"*? This stage is very much like a new business making a decision on what they are going to sell in the marketplace. As a mentor for entrepreneurs, I'm constantly working with ambitious individuals who have a ton of ideas for a business. Some of those aspiring entrepreneurs have ideas that are so vast that there is not a singular focus in their early planning stage. As a result of this broad idea, business planning with these individuals can be difficult. However, once I get these individuals to focus on a primary idea and purpose, planning for their future business venture becomes much easier.

Deciding your true purpose requires honest, and sometimes painful, self-analysis. I say it is sometimes painful because in self-analysis, if done with an honest lens, one can come to the realization that something that they thought they loved to do or something that they were really good at doing, they are not actually good at, at all. This self-reflection can sometimes be depressing. All things considered, self-analysis can also be wonderful because it helps a person really get in touch with one's true self. Once one is in touch with their true self, they are better equipped to determine their purpose.

Once you have determined your purpose, it is wise to then determine your brand. In marketing, brand awareness is important because the brand is what you're known for. Mercedes Benz is a car company known for building quality/luxurious vehicles. When you see the emblem, you're automatically thinking about a vehicle that is of high quality and possibly high price. For decades, quality and luxury were the top two words associated with Mercedes-Benz. However, in the late 80s and early 90s, Mercedes decided to come out with a "cheap" entry-level model. A model in which everyone could afford. As a result of this new model, many loyal Mercedes-Benz customers moved on from Mercedes and decided to buy other luxury brands. When asked why they left Mercedes, those customers said that Mercedes had stepped away from luxury and prestige, and those customers purchased their Mercedes as a mark of their status.

Though the vast majority of you will not be going out to build luxury cars, you will be actively promoting and selling your purpose to family, friends and organizations. Your brand is your reputation, your brand is a thing that others consider your expertise. It is important that you understand your brand, build your brand, and maintain the integrity of your brand.

Finally, there is loyalty. We all have a product or brand in which we are loyal. I play beer league hockey, and I am extremely loyal to the Bauer brand. Bauer has done a great job at marketing to amateur hockey players. They even have a product line of skates, sticks, and other equipment specifically designed towards amateur and entry-level players. My brand loyalty has extended to buying T-shirts, hats, and other items that advertise the Bauer brand. As a result, my loyalty has given Bauer an added channel of promotion.

Though people may not be wearing items with your name on it, it is important that you are loyal and promote your "brand". I'm not saying that you should be braggadocious, but I am saying that you should find humble ways to promote yourself. That could be simply volunteering for a community organization, or being a part of a social organization and providing some type of skilled service. The best way to promote your brand is through humble actions and not arrogant words.

Purpose

Now since you have considered the product, brand, and loyalty, let's start on refining your path. That path obviously starts with purpose. The Oxford Dictionary has two definitions for purpose: one is a noun, the other is a verb. The noun for purpose is "the reason for which something is done or created or for which something exists". This book will dive into depth with both definitions.

First, let's talk about *"the reason for which something is done, created or for which something exists"*. Have you ever asked yourself, *"Why do you exist?"* This question can be a very difficult one to answer. This question is an extremely difficult answer if your life is going through a period of transition. Though it was so many years ago, I remember my high school graduation back in 1989. I could not wait for the Superintendent of the Williamsville, (New York) Central School District to call my name, so I could go up on the stage and receive my diploma. The smile on my face was extremely large when I heard my name and was handed my diploma. As I was walking off that stage, I remember feeling a sense of dread. Since I was five years old, my primary existence was to be a student and I existed to learn. However, once I received the diploma, for some reason, I realized that my existence was more complicated and involved. The dread I felt was that I didn't know at the time my other reasons for existence. It was at that very moment that I realized I was uncertain of my purpose.

I know that now since I am able to look back and I'm much, much older. Back then I did not have a clue of what was happening to me, and I spent many years floating through life, barely getting by, and not serving my purpose. It wasn't until I joined the Navy that I realized that a good life was not by chance but purposeful design. It is possible that anyone can create a good life, regardless of their circumstance. Though it is not always easy, with a clearly defined purpose, one can make their life mostly what they want it to be.

In order to set the course for a good life, you must understand your purpose. Keep in mind that your purpose does change as your life changes. For example, from 1971, up until about 1994, my mother and father's purpose with my younger brother and I was to feed, cloth, and house us. However, once we graduated high school and started lives of our own, the purpose of my parents changed. They both became my greatest advisors. When I got out of the Navy and started my career in higher education, I would call my mother in the morning on the way to work to get her encouragement to approach my day with hope and confidence. At the end of the day, on my way home, I would call my father for my reality check. Those daily calls were very valuable to me. They would not have been if my parents did not realize that their roles have changed. Realizing when it is time to alter your purpose can be challenging, and we will devote time to that soon.

Knowing your purpose requires a great deal of self-reflection. During self-reflection, you must understand the following: your role in the lives of others, what you truly want in life, your current stage in life, what you want out of life, what your current place is in life and what you desire your future place in life to be. You may not have an answer to all of these questions right now. The subsequent chapters of this book are designed to assist in answering each and every one of these questions.

Chapter 3

Your Role in the Lives of Others

One of the greatest privileges I got to experience was to coach my two sons' little league hockey team. I started coaching this team about three months after my daughter was murdered. Going to the rink with my two sons, and spending quality time with them, was an outlet for both them and me. The team was a hodgepodge of kids with varied levels of skill. However, one thing the team had was a lot of heart. As a result of their heart and desire, our team went 22 and 1. Unfortunately, the only game we lost was the All-City championship which was an interleague competition to determine who was the champion of Indianapolis. I still have the medal and trophy from that season. I still have the team picture. That team represented much more than 10 and 11-year-olds playing hockey. That team was symbolic of finding joy in victory even in your darkest times.

The reason I bring up this hockey team is because of an incident that happened before the game one Saturday morning. The assistant coach and I were in the locker room with the team discussing strategy. Some of the players were still putting on their equipment when a mother walked into the locker room, unannounced to tie her son's skates. I remember telling this parent that she was not authorized to be in the locker room at that time. Her reply was that her son did not know how to tie his skates, and would fall and hurt himself if she didn't tie them.

I remember looking at that boy's face. He was highly embarrassed to be around other 10 to 12-year-old boys who did know how to tie their skates. There clearly was a moment of awkwardness. I replied to the mother that we would assist her son in tying the skates. However, I walked out of the locker room with her and said that though we would assist in tying his skates, he would be doing most of the tying on his own. The mother was rather miffed, but she did go back to the stands to wait for her son's game to start. I could say that this young player tied his skates perfectly without incident. However, that would be a lie.

With only my verbal instruction, the young man tied his skates. However, just like the mother said, he did not tie them tight enough. As a result of his loose-fitting skates, the young man fell rather hard into the boards, and I had to walk out to escort him back to the bench. I remember looking in the stands and seeing the absolute disgust of the mother. I also remember telling the boy that when he got back to the bench to do exactly what I told him to, to tie his skates extra tight. About three minutes later, the boy said he was ready to go back on the ice and his skates were tight. They were so tight that at the end of the game, it was necessary for him to get assistance to untie them.

THE 4P'S OF YOU

The boy felt a level of confidence and satisfaction when he realized that he could tie his own skates effectively. Clearly, his role as a young child officially ended that day, and his new role as an aspiring young man started. On the other hand, his mother's role changed as well. She no longer had to do everything for the child. There were clearly some things that this young man was clearly capable of doing on his own.

In this story, because the mother did not realize her changing role, she ended up doing too much for her son. Because she did not acknowledge her duties in her role as a mother must decrease, this mother unintentionally impeded on her son's role and purpose to increase. In both personal and professional environments, this understanding of their role can interfere with the growth and success of the entire process.

Just as doing too much in your role can interfere with the process, doing too little can be damaging as well. Some years back, I decided to follow the money and accept a job as a Business Chair and regional accreditation member for a struggling for-profit college. In hindsight, this was not the greatest of career decisions, but the financial compensation that came with the position was more than overly tempting. I took the job and was professionally disappointed within three months.

The principal reason for disappointment was a complete lack of direction. The president/CEO of this college succeeded his father. His father was a visionary, understood the purpose of the college and cared deeply for not only the success of the institution, but the success of all those who graduated. It was not unheard of to watch this man cleaning up the cafeteria and emptying out the trash cans after students left the cafeteria. His drive and his purpose made the college successful. Though the father was phenomenal at conveying the purpose and mission of the school to students and faculty, he was not as successful conveying that purpose to the son.

The son and new CEO of the college understood his role to be showing up to college, functions of pomp and circumstance and being very hands-off in mission and function of the college as a whole. As a result, vice presidents and "lieutenants" of the college started developing their own purpose, and that purpose was not singular, but divided into departmental and self-interest of several people. As a result of the CEO's lack of focus, the college lost its direction. In some cases, whether intentional or not, the college started implementing unethical practices that severely damaged their students. Educators who saw the internal destruction of the college started moving on to other positions at other colleges and universities. Eventually, the college closed down in disgrace leaving hundreds of students without a degree, and with college credits that were nearly worthless.

The case of the mother who did not know when to reduce her role, thus interfering with her son's growth, the case of the CEO who didn't know how to increase his role caused those around them to prematurely increase their role. This premature growth of those around the CEO led to the entire organization, not growing at all. It is imperative that there is balance in your role, and all of your roles holistically, must be achieved.

Back in the early 2000s, I had the esteemed pleasure of being a Navy recruiter. I absolutely loved that job. One of the reasons I did enjoy the job so much is because of my Zone Supervisor NCC Buck Campfield. Chief Campfield was at the end of his career, and Navy Reserve Recruiting Command Area Central, which eventually became Navy Recruiting District Indianapolis, which eventually became Navy Recruiting District Michigan would be his last duty station before retiring.

It is very common for those tail end of their career, regardless of whether it's military or civilian, to kind of take on a nonchalant attitude and not care about many aspects of their job due to the fact that they're really not going to be around for a long time to experience either the positive or negative effects of what's going on around them. However, this was not Campfield's attitude at all. As a matter fact, it was the direct opposite. His actions showed me that Campfield used his last duty station as one last-ditch effort to make the United States Navy even better than it was when he joined. It was an absolute blessing that my path, and the path of my fellow shipmates that worked for him happened to cross.

Buck Campfield embraced his purpose of being an outstanding United States sailor, and he truly understood that his role had evolved into that of more of a mentor to younger sailors. Buck Campfield supervised Navy recruiters in the states of Indiana and Cincinnati, Ohio. The total number under his charge was roughly 25 sailors. Under his leadership, a vast majority of the sailors experienced tremendous growth professionally. One of the sailors went on to become a Master Chief, another became a Senior Chief, four that I know of became Chiefs.

Campfield also stressed the importance of higher education. When I first met Chief Campfield, I did not have a higher education credential. However, one day the chief was talking to me one-on-one and in that conversation, he complimented me on my hard work and dedication to recruiting. He then stated that he was retiring soon and getting a civilian job, and if my resume crossed his desk, he would not hire me because I had an opportunity to get a college degree for free and refused to do so. I remember how that conversation made me feel. Frankly, I was angry. The very next day I went to Marian College and enrolled in their adult program. By the time I got out of the Navy, I was one semester shy of completing my Masters degree.

Because he knew his role and his purpose, Chief Campfield led his sailors to become a very successful unit for Navy Recruiting District Area Central. His example helped his subordinates gain a better understanding of their purpose. Honestly, I don't think I would be where I am today if it wasn't for Buck Campfield. I am confident that many of the other sailors I served with under his command would express the same.

If you, as a leader, in whatever capacity that may be, understand your purpose and your role, those around you begin to understand their purpose and their role. There is a balance, there is a harmony that develops. This is true in any circumstance. If you are confident and balanced in your role as a mother, your children are more likely to become more stable and balanced. If you are more confident and balanced in your role and purpose as a manager, those who work under you will gain confidence and balance as well. Balance is not easy to maintain, but it is manageable.

Constant purpose changing role

When I speak of balance between purpose and role, this is what I mean. Let's go back to the mother who came into the hockey locker room to tie her child's skates. I'm quite confident that her number one purpose was to be the most supportive and loving mother she possibly could be to her children. And based on my interaction with her in the family, I have no reason to doubt her purpose. When it comes to her being a fantastic mother, that purpose will never change. However, as time goes by, her role as a mother will change several times. The trick is knowing when the role has changed.

Not knowing when your role has changed can lead to chaos and embarrassment. Back in 2005, the Green Bay Packers drafted Aaron Rodgers to be heir apparent to quarterback great Brett Favre. In the very beginning, Aaron Rodgers sat patiently on the bench and accepted the tutelage of Brett Favre on the ins and outs of the NFL game. In 2007, the leadership of the Green Bay Packers decided that it was time for the roles to change, and Aaron Rodgers should now take what he learned from Brett Favre and be the Packers starting quarterback while Brett Favre mentored from the bench. Brett Favre refused to accept that role. As a result, one of the most accomplished quarterbacks in NFL history experienced a rather unceremonious exit from a franchise and a fan base that grew to love him.

Brett Favre went on to play for the Minnesota Vikings and the New York Jets. Though he did experience success in Minnesota, his time in New York was rather tumultuous. Brett Favre was reluctant to give up his role as a star quarterback. He did not want to accept his role as a mentor. As a result, his purpose of being a great quarterback was slightly tarnished due to his reluctance to fully understand his changing role.

The question is: would Brett Favre still be known as one of the greatest quarterbacks in NFL history if he would've spent his last two NFL seasons backing up and mentoring Aaron Rodgers? I would venture to say the answer is *"yes"*. However, because Favre did not want to accept his changing role, though accomplishments on the field cannot be denied, Brett Favre is often the subject to *"retire/unretired"* off-color jokes.

Oftentimes someone's purpose is a constant. Like all fathers, I strive to be a great father. The father who was always there for his children. My oldest *"child"* is now 27 years old. My role in his life has changed several times during those 27 years. I will admit that sometimes the role changed before I realized that it had changed, but nonetheless it's changed. Time has an ever-evolving impact on one's role and a steady but slower impact on one's purpose. The hardest part with a constant purpose and the changing role is maintaining balance.

To make balance even more complicated, one must balance multiple roles. If you want to simplify, most of us have two roles: one is professional, and the other is personal. But if you take a deeper look, your professional can have several secondary and tertiary roles that follow. Professionally, for example, you may be a person in middle management. Just right there you are a leader and manager of some and a follower insubordinate of others. Within an 8- to 12-hour day, you can change your role many, many times. For those who must do this daily, I do not have to tell you how difficult that may be. Understanding your role(s) holistically can help in balancing your purpose.

The fact of the matter is we serve multiple roles daily. As community members and leaders, we are employees, we are employers, we are customers, family members, friends, and citizens. One can simply go from one conversation to the next and change roles three times. Balancing roles in a way that serves your purpose can be extremely difficult. One must always remember that a decision you make will almost certainly have an impact on every other role you serve.

When recognizing the roles, it is important to set a priority on those roles. In other words, roles must be categorized and prioritized in order of importance and impact. For example, my roles as husband and father take priority over every other role I serve. So, with that in mind, I must remember that every decision I make, regardless of the role, can have an effect on my role as a husband and father.

Let's go back to the decision I made when I came to the conclusion that I wasn't serving my purpose. I decided that it was healthy for me to take a pay cut and leave a comfortable paying college administration job. I also decided it would ultimately be healthy for my entire family if my marriage ended. Both of those decisions affected every single role I had, and it also had an effect on those who were influenced and impacted by the roles I served. Decisions made by individuals are not made in a vacuum. When it comes to staying in tune with your purpose, it is imperative that the positive and negative effects of every decision must be considered.

THE 4P'S OF YOU

Self-reflection

It is imperative to take time for self-reflection. Back when I worked at the now-defunct college, I had a lot on my plate. I was the department chair, I was still working on my PhD dissertation, I was consulting an entrepreneur in his launching of a new business venture, and I was trying to spend ample time with my family who was going through a lot of transition. I put myself in a position where I had spread myself way too thin. So thin that I started to lose sleep and the stress was not sitting well with my mental well-being. I decided to go and talk to my pastor at the time to see if he knew how I could destress.

During our meeting, my cell phone rang countless times. Some of the calls I could ignore, but some of the calls could not be ignored. Finally, my pastor looked at me and said that I was solving too many problems off-the-cuff and eventually that would wind up helping no one. He also said that while I was in his office trying to obtain mental clarity for myself, I was allowing others to interfere with that process thus possibly creating an unclear situation and circumstance for those who rely on me. He also stated that it is important for someone's physical and mental well-being to take time on a regular basis to self-reflect, recharge, and rest.

The best way to be effective in your role, become your purpose, and serve others effectively is to take time for yourself. I know I do most of my self-reflection through exercise. I go on long bike rides by myself. While I'm on the trails, I'm thinking and reflecting on several different situations going on in my life professionally and personally. I also drive quite a bit, and while driving longer distances I take that time for reflection as well. In addition, I also play hockey on a weekly basis, both on roller and on ice. During the hour or hour and a half, I am on the ice, I am only thinking about the game. Everyone needs a little bit of mindless time. Quite frankly hockey empties my mind just enough to make room for important ideas. Some of my best decisions are made after spending time in a *"relaxed"* environment created by my time at the rink.

Exercise/self-reflection and my rink time also help me in recognizing what I truly want in life. During self-reflection, I often ask myself: Am I on track? Am I serving my purpose? Are the steps I'm taking truly taking me to where I want and what I want? Knowing what you want is almost as important as understanding your roles. This is yet another thing to consider when determining your purpose.

Chapter 4

What Do You Want?

Because of a program created by the state of Indiana, I am fortunate to assist in helping state inmates find stable career employment after they get out of prison. My role in this program is to conduct a course in which I help inmates plan for life after prison. The course deals with accepting personal responsibility, better decision-making, and developing a solid personal and professional life plan.

On the first day of class, I always ask my new students, *"What do you want when you get out of prison?"*. The initial answer from all of those students is almost identical. They will say that they want to get a good job. That they want to stay away from the way of life that got them in prison in the first place. And they also want a place of their own so they can take care of their families and the ones that they love. My response to them is always, *"Yes, but what do you really want?"* At that point, the whole room will go silent. The room would go silent because most of the time these students did not know exactly what I was asking.

No matter who we are, or where we are in life, we all want a good job, we all want to make good decisions that keep us out of trouble, and we all want to provide for our loved ones in the best way possible. The problem lies in describing what those look like, and how to create the environment in which your vision becomes a reality. Oftentimes we neglect to properly reflect and act upon building that reality.

During the class I conduct with inmates, I help each and every one of them create and plan for the life that they truly want to live. The foundation of that creation is recognizing what those inmates truly want. For example, when they state that they want a place of their own, where is that place? Is it a place where there is a good school system? Is it a place where there is access to opportunities in their desired career field? Like these inmates in my class, detailing your wants is essential to finding and serving your purpose.

Details, details, details

Whenever I consult small businesses, the first thing I ask the entrepreneur is *"Where do you see your business in five years?"*. If that entrepreneur cannot answer this question with some level of clarity, then I tell the business owner that I cannot properly consult their organization until they have some idea as to where they are going. I mostly will spend the rest of that meeting brainstorming about the future. In some cases, I will have a follow-up meeting to start the consulting process. However, in other cases, I don't meet with that organization again.

Vision, purpose, and desires have a major influence on your direction. In order to truly satisfy your purpose, you must know what you want. Your purpose and your wants must align with each other. That alignment will then assist in the organization of your actions. By having a vague idea of what you want, there is a very good chance that you will not necessarily make the right steps in achieving your purpose in accomplishing your goals. You must be specific and detailed in what you want.

Let's go back to the story of my inmates who are about ready to get out of prison. When I ask them what they want, they respond with wanting to make money, legally, wanting to take care of their family, and never wanting to go back to prison. However, when I asked them what that looks like, there's always a blank stare. They don't know what I mean. Quite frankly, there are a lot of individuals who may not know exactly what I mean when I ask that question.

For clarity, here is what I meant when I asked that question *"What does it look like"*. When I ask an inmate about a job that they desire to have, I want to know what is the task, salary, and profession you envision. When I ask them what they mean by taking care of their family, I want to know are they simply paying child support, or are they spending time with them, or are they living with them. These are details that we all must consider when considering what we want. We must be specific!

Specifics in your wants apply to tangible and intangible items. For example, you may want to car. However, what is that car going to look like? Is a car going to be a compact car or an SUV?

What colors is the car going to be? Do you want comfort, or do you want gas mileage? If you don't answer questions like that, you may very well select the wrong car and have buyer's remorse. And with the price and length of car loans in this day and age, that remorse will last for 48 to 72 months. Make sure you do your research, recognize what is the purpose of the vehicle, how long are you going to keep the vehicle, and how much are you willing to pay on a monthly basis for that vehicle. Those specific questions and features, if answered correctly will lead you to making the proper decisions.

My previous example of the car purchase is a tangible aspect of personal wants. There are also many, and I do mean many, intangible aspects of personal wants. Those intangible aspects are things like personal satisfaction, feeling of belonging, being loved, and having joy. When it comes to intangible wants, there is a great deal of self-reflection that is needed. For example, when it comes to wanting joy, one must realize that there is a difference between joy and happiness. Happiness is fleeting while joy is a permanent feeling.

My children give me a great sense of joy. Every time I think of them, feel I love that I've never experienced or felt in my life. However, they do not always make me happy. Like every parent, I do have stories of when my children have wrecked cars, snuck out of the house, and messed up in school. Each of those instances clearly did not make me happy. However, I would not change one single moment with my children due to the fact that each experience whether it makes me happy or unhappy always adds to the joy of the privilege of being a parent.

The difference between joy and happiness is just one example when it comes to the details of your wants. Sometimes it is more difficult to determine your intangible wants from your tangible wants. Once again, it is important to truly ask yourself what it is you truly want.

Though it may be hard for some to determine their personal intangible wants, it may be easier to determine intangible wants when it comes to your professional goals. When talking to students about their potential career choices, it almost comes natural for students to make their career choices based on intangible wants and job satisfaction. When I talk to students who want to be in the medical field, students almost immediately say it is their desire to help people that drove them to that particular career choice. The feeling one may get when helping others is indeed intangible; you can't really see it nor can you describe it. However, that feeling leads to job satisfaction almost immediately.

When it comes to professional wants, quite frankly you want a career that whenever you get paid you almost feel that you are taking your employer's money. You want to have a career where if given the circumstances or the opportunity you would do that job for free. I knew of a teacher back in Brazil, Indiana who taught math to seventh and eighth graders. When that man retired, he continued to be active in tutoring middle school students in the community. He tutored those kids for free. He was truly a blessing to every individual who had the opportunity to be taught by him. Clearly, there was a joy and a passion that he found in teaching that stayed with him until his very last breath. Teaching young men and women was clearly what he wanted to do. And though he was a local businessman, he owned the Dairy Queen in town, he will always be known as what he wanted to be known as and that is an outstanding teacher.

Many equate professional success with lots of money. That is definitely not always the case. When it comes to wants and professional success, one must be very careful to find the right balance between financial prosperity and professional satisfaction. Throughout my lifetime I have seen many financially successful individuals who were simply measurable professionally. Once again, professional wants and goals should always be something that one really desires to do. It's a shame to see successful individuals grow to regret their professional decisions many years after they have committed to a professional path. Worse yet, it is horrible to see people who are at the end of their life regret that they did not take advantage of other opportunities that were presented to them. Unfortunately, I witnessed that regret firsthand back in 2013.

Two days before the death of my father in November 2013, my stepmother walked into my dad's hospital room after working all day at the family skating rink. My stepmother walked over to my father's bed and asked him if he wanted to know how the skating session went that day. My father shook his head "no" basically indicating through his body language that he never wanted to hear about his beloved skating rink for the rest of his life. I know from some of the conversations I had with my father while he was in hospice, there are so many other things that he wanted to do professionally. However, the financial success that came from the skating rink and the nightclub that was upstairs distracted him from other entrepreneurial endeavors. My father taught me a valuable lesson from these conversations that though money is important to obtaining a certain lifestyle, it is clearly not the ultimate measure of professional success.

It is imperative to have both professional and personal wants. Over time, your wants will change due to your age, your status in life, and the environment around you. Regardless of how much or how many times your wants both professionally and personally change, it is imperative that you maintain the proper balance between professional and personal goals and wants. It is important that your professional and personal goals are in line with your primary purpose. An imbalance between your wants can totally distract you and drive you away from your purpose.

I always wanted to provide for my family. I wanted to give them everything I could. Like the majority of parents, I wanted my children to have a great life. The Navy provided me with the financial means to serve my purpose of being the best father I can be. During this time in the Navy, I was able to buy a home in a very nice neighborhood in Indianapolis and provide my children with all of the amenities necessary to live a comfortable life. During my time as a recruiter in the Navy, I recall spending a lot of time at the office and away from my family. This had an effect on my oldest daughter.

From time to time my oldest daughter would come to work with me at the Naval Reserve station. The XO of the duty station at the time had a daughter the same age as mine, and they became close friends. However, my job still required me to be away from home quite a bit. I received several awards and accolades for my time as a military recruiter.

In June 2015, my oldest daughter was shot while trying to break up a fight. I remember being notified and quickly going to the crime scene. I had to stand there for several hours waiting for the coroner to arrive so I could officially identify my daughter's body. I vaguely remember some of the random thoughts that went through my head while I was waiting. One of those thoughts was recalling my oldest daughter telling me as a young child that she hated my job because I was away from home so much. This was the most extreme example of, at least at that time, not having an adequate balance between my personal and professional wants. There are many days that I go back and wish that I could fix that balance. Clearly the only thing I can do is take steps to avoid imbalances like that in the future. I can also warn you the reader to avoid something like this happening in your life.

One of the best ways to avoid that imbalance is through journaling and self-reflection. If you haven't noticed by now, self-reflection will be a theme in this book when it comes to purpose. The best thing you can do is take time out of every day to analyze your current place. Always make sure that you are on the right track. Be honest with yourself. I do that by looking straight in the mirror before I go to bed every night. I ask myself *"Did I do all I could do today to achieve my goals in the future"*. One thing you cannot do is look yourself dead in the eye and lie to yourself. If I answer that question with a *"yes"*, then I end the day with satisfaction. If I answer that question with a *"no"*, then I make sure that the first thing I do the following morning is to develop a plan to get back on schedule.

Is it what you want?

At Ivy Tech Community College I teach a class that helps students adjust to college life. There is a section of the course that deals with deciding future careers. Usually at the beginning of this section, I go to each student in the class and ask them what career they want after college. In one class I remember asking a student what she wanted to do, and she replied that she wanted to be a nurse. I asked her why she wanted to be a nurse. She responded because her mother was a nurse. I asked her again why she wanted to be a nurse. She responded once more because her mother was a nurse. I then asked her one more time why she wanted to be a nurse. Her response the final time was *"I want to be a teacher"*. She was making a decision not on her, but on her family's legacy. The student in the story did eventually change majors, and she became an outstanding elementary school teacher.

If the student in my story became a nurse, I am confident that she would have been a very good nurse. I am also confident that that student would later in life regret not pursuing her dream of becoming an elementary school teacher. When deciding what you want out of life, make sure it is truly what you want. If you are pursuing what others want out of your life, you are ultimately pursuing someone else's purpose. When pursuing someone else's purpose, you will ultimately lose passion. Without passion, it is quite possible for your success to seem empty.

Don't settle

Equally important to making sure that your wants are indeed your wants is to make sure that you don't automatically settle for less than what you want. Yes, there is a level of compromise with anything, but automatically settling for less than what you work for ultimately leads to misery. My father owned a nightclub in Buffalo, New York for over 40 years. Back when he owned the nightclub, bars, and nightclubs in Buffalo closed at 4 AM. Every night at 2 AM, my father would walk back to the DJ booth, get on the microphone, and say, *"It's 2 o'clock, it's time for you to forget what you came for and take what you can get"*. Clearly, he was referring to a love connection or a hookup. What is funny is that there were indeed people at the bar who would start talking to people that they normally wouldn't talk to, and there were some cases where those two individuals left the bar together. I am quite confident that in more cases than not both of those individuals woke up the next morning regretting that they took my father's advice.

Today several years later, Trunnis Sr.'s son is now stating that you do not settle. Always remember what you came for, you work hard enough, never willingly settle for less than what you deserve. When it comes to your personal life never take a, take what you can get attitude. Sometimes you may have to work harder, but always remember you're not a nightclub and there is no closing time. It is never too late to get what you truly desire. Though it may take extra effort, reaching your goals and desires is worth the reward.

That goes professionally as well. I have seen a lot of individuals settle for jobs beneath their qualifications because they may have settled for security. I've seen others settle for professions because they were not willing to make the sacrifices that were necessary, such as moving to a different city or obtaining certain credentials, that were necessary to make in order to be in the profession they desire.

Remember you should always treat yourself in a way in which you feel comfortable in getting what you truly deserve. Do not discount yourself in any way that takes away rewards that you deserve to have. Instead of taking what you can get, strive for what you earn. Life will clearly be more satisfying once you adopt that philosophy.

Chapter 5

The Evolution of Purpose

When I released the first edition of this book, I hosted several book launch events that were filled with heartfelt stories, engaging conversations, and unforgettable moments. One particularly memorable event took place in Indiana. During that event, an individual in the audience asked me a profound and thought-provoking question: *"Can purpose change?"* At the time, my response was confident and unwavering. I believed that while purpose could evolve and deepen with time and experience, once an individual found it, their core purpose rarely changed entirely.

However, that belief would soon be challenged in the most unexpected and humbling way. Through my work, I had the honor of meeting two remarkable women: Dr. Angela Bennett and Ms. Tessa Williams. Both of these incredible individuals hail from Australia—a country where the sex industry is not only legalized in many regions but is also deeply woven into the cultural and economic fabric. At one point in their lives, both Dr. Bennett and Ms. Williams were highly successful participants in this industry. Financially, they prospered, but emotionally and spiritually, they were burdened with trauma and addiction—wounds that defy easy explanation.

I had the opportunity to meet these women after they had made the courageous decision to leave the sex industry. It was during a recent business trip and conference in Australia that I was introduced to their stories. Getting to know them over time has been nothing short of transformative for me. I now count them among my closest and most inspirational friends. Their lives serve as vivid testaments to the power of purpose not just to evolve, but to be completely reimagined.

Even during their time in the sex industry, they carried themselves with a unique sense of discipline, integrity, and focus. For example, Ms. Williams was once regarded as the 'Queen of Dominatrix' in her field—a title that came with prestige and financial reward. Yet, behind the confidence and success, there was a persistent inner turmoil. Beneath the surface lay deeply rooted trauma, emotional scars, and an unshakable feeling of emptiness. The life they lived may have offered them control over others, but it failed to deliver peace within themselves.

Dr. Bennett's transformation began with a painful journey through addiction and emotional isolation. The road to healing was steep and unsteady, but she found her strength through her unwavering faith in Jesus Christ and the steadfast love of her family. With time, grace, and commitment, she stepped away from her former life and embraced a new one centered on healing, advocacy, and empowerment. Similarly, Ms. Williams experienced a defining moment of reckoning when she realized that her influence, once admired in the realm she operated in, was now contributing to a culture of distorted sexual expectations among young men. This realization struck her deeply and changed her forever.

Dr. Bennett has since built a new life defined not by her past but by her renewed sense of purpose. She is now a loving grandmother who cherishes the simple, sacred joys of family life. She launched a powerful ministry aimed at helping women transition out of the sex industry and reclaim their lives. Her latest venture, Esther's House, is a nonprofit organization based in Australia that provides comprehensive support services including addiction recovery, safe housing, employment pathways, and trauma healing. The foundation is a lighthouse for women navigating their way out of darkness.

Ms. Williams's journey of transformation was more public and, at times, more turbulent. When she transitioned into a new role focused on children and education, her past drew unwanted attention from the media. Critics sought to sensationalize her story, turning her efforts into tabloid fodder. But with courage, faith, and the unwavering support of her church community, she rose above the noise. Today, she is not only a committed academic and Sunday school teacher but also a role model for women and girls navigating their own paths of recovery.

What both women demonstrate so clearly is that the process of stepping into a new purpose often demands immense sacrifice. It means confronting societal judgment, letting go of financial security, and surrendering a former identity in exchange for one that may not yet be fully formed. For Dr. Bennett, it meant rebuilding her life from the ground up, guided by faith and humility. For Ms. Williams, it meant risking public scrutiny to pursue a calling she knew was greater than her past. Their lives reflect an unyielding perseverance that is not only admirable—it is instructive.

I remember a conversation I had with Ms. Williams that particularly stood out. She spoke about the harsh labels imposed on her during childhood by people she once admired in the church community. One person even called her *'evil,'* a label that clung to her for years. Over time, she began to internalize that judgment and decided to embody the identity others had unfairly crafted for her. That distorted perception of purpose—one born out of shame and rejection—ultimately led her down a path of self-sabotage. Her journey reminds us of the importance of forming an authentic purpose based on self-discovery, not others' expectations.

This pattern—of individuals adopting roles based on how they are perceived rather than who they truly are—is not unique to Ms. Williams. It is a recurring theme in many of the stories I have come across. One of the most powerful examples is my friend Jeff Hanlan, a driven and successful social entrepreneur based in Toronto. Jeff's early life was marked by hardship, particularly due to the incarceration of his father. As a result, he grew up in a world that frequently judged him by his circumstances rather than his character.

Jeff's story took a dramatic turn when he was involved in a life-threatening incident that forced him to confront the path he was on. That moment of crisis became a catalyst for change. Today, Jeff is a leader and mentor who collaborates with well-established nonprofit organizations across Canada. He uses his lived experience to inspire youth, build community programs, and foster hope in marginalized communities. He is living proof that even when the world tells you who you are, you can rewrite your narrative and forge a new purpose.

So, to return to the question posed in Indiana—can purpose change? Without a doubt, the answer is yes. The lives of Angela, Tessa, and Jeff illustrate this truth vividly. Purpose not only can change, but sometimes it must. Life has a way of teaching us, reshaping us, and refining the lens through which we see our role in the world. And when those lessons come, the real question becomes: are we brave enough to answer the call?

Purpose, like any meaningful journey, requires work. It demands reflection, a willingness to face painful truths, and the ability to pivot when we discover that what once served us may no longer align with who we are. To change one's purpose is not to betray it—but to elevate it. It is to honor growth, to recognize that the road ahead may be different, but it is no less worthy.

The evolution of purpose is not just a possibility—it is a gift. One that allows us to continue becoming the people we were truly meant to be.

Chapter 6

You Can't Force Purpose

Purpose is not something that can be manufactured or forced into existence. It must emerge through patience, experience, and honest self-reflection. For those familiar with my brother David's book, **Can't Hurt Me**, you know that our upbringing was far from idyllic. Unlike the wholesome families portrayed in shows like **The Brady Bunch**, **Leave It to Beaver**, or **Good Times**, my childhood home was filled with conflict and instability. I don't mention this to evoke sympathy but to provide context. As a child, I imagined a different kind of family life—one I wasn't sure was even possible until I met TJ McAfoos.

I met TJ during one of the most isolating times in my life. My parents had just separated, and I had relocated to a new town where I didn't know anyone. Emotionally lost and socially disconnected, I met TJ at the local park pool in Brazil, Indiana. Though I didn't feel like talking to anyone that day, TJ made it his mission to introduce himself. Surprisingly, we hit it off immediately and became inseparable for years.

TJ's parents, Rod and Linda McAfoos, modeled the kind of family I had always dreamed of. They were warm, consistent, and clearly committed to one another. Their marriage wasn't perfect, but it was real—and it endured. Over time, I came to admire them deeply and began to believe that having a family like theirs could be part of my own future. It was a beautiful vision, but one that I unfortunately began to force.

When you force your purpose—personally or professionally—you invite unintended consequences. I believed my purpose was to replicate the McAfoos family model. Driven by that belief, I entered into marriages not grounded in readiness or compatibility, but in an idealized vision. The result was painful: three divorces, emotional distress, and heartbreak for not only myself and my ex-wives but also my children. I did my best to maintain open communication with their mothers, and I worked hard to prevent them from experiencing the same childhood instability I had, but the damage of forcing that vision was real.

This pattern didn't end with my personal life. I also forced my professional purpose. While I was serving as a faculty lead at Western Governors University—a role I genuinely loved—I became fixated on advancement. I accepted a department chair position at a college I knew had red flags. The title and perceived prestige clouded my judgment. Within a short period, that institution shut down, and I not only lost the position—I had to return to the classroom as a standard faculty member. Ironically, that experience reminded me how much I loved teaching, and it helped me rediscover my true calling.

The desire to grow and evolve is natural and commendable. But pushing forward without the necessary preparation can lead to setbacks that take years to recover from. Purpose has its own timing, and it often unfolds when we least expect it—but when we are finally ready.

One of the key strategies to avoid forcing purpose is to build a support system of people who can keep you grounded. As someone with a Type A personality, impatience has always been my Achilles heel. I am currently training for a CrossFit competition that will take place in Sydney, Australia 2026. Being well over 50 years old, this is a new and challenging endeavor for me. While I have the strength and stamina from years of daily workouts, I lack technical mastery in many CrossFit disciplines. Thankfully, I have a trainer who understands my mindset and keeps my ambition in check.

The truth is, you need honest voices in your life—people who will tell you, 'Not yet,' even when you're eager to hear 'Go.' Whether in relationships, career paths, or personal goals, timing matters. The people around you should be those who are not only supportive but also honest and experienced enough to help you slow down when necessary.

Another essential step is to recognize that purpose is a journey made up of incremental milestones. You don't simply wake up and decide your purpose; it is revealed through actions, setbacks, discipline, and progress. There are steps—often unseen by others—that must be taken to build the foundation for meaningful purpose. Skipping those steps leads to false starts and frustration.

In retrospect, I often reflect on how much pain could have been avoided if I had simply been more patient. My journey toward building a successful family didn't begin until I stopped trying to recreate someone else's life and instead focused on understanding my own. Today, I am grateful to say that I have a loving, supportive family. But the road to get here was filled with unnecessary detours caused by my own impatience.

Purpose is not an on-demand achievement. It is a slow burn, a deeply personal calling that must be nurtured, not rushed. In fact, if I were to revisit the title of my book **The 4P's of You**, I might be tempted to add a fifth 'P'—Patience. Without it, none of the others—Purpose, Planning, Passion, and Persistence—can fully flourish.

Chapter 7

It's All in the Planning

Back in 2000, Tim Meadows starred in an entertaining comedy that was based on a Saturday Night Live skit titled, The Ladies Man. In this movie, Tim's character, Leon Phelps, was a womanizing radio talk show host who lost his job due to being very vulgar on the air. His radio producer, Julie Simmons, played by Karyn Parsons, was fired as well. For most of the movie, Leon and Julie went from radio station to radio station to find a job. All the while, Leon Phelps was trying to find a woman who was wealthy who had written a letter to him stating that she was going to leave her husband and run away with Leon and spend all of her husband's money. She signed the letter *"your Sweet Thang"*. Little did she know that Leon was *"Sweet Thang"*.

In one scene of this movie, Julie got frustrated with Leon due to the fact that Leon was not really focused on the task of finding a new radio job. After getting fired once more from a radio station, Julie has had enough and is just about to give up on Leon. At the moment Julie was walking away, Leon said with absolute confidence *"I am going to sit back and wait for something randomly to happen"*. The funny part is something really did randomly happen, and Julie and Leon eventually wound up living happily ever after. Though sitting back and relying on random events to work his way worked for Leon Phelps, it hardly ever works for anyone else.

In order to serve your purpose and reach your goals, it is imperative that you create a well thought out plan.

From the time I was 18 years old until the time I was about 23, I basically lived my life like Leon Phelps. However, when I look back at that time, I really don't see anything too funny. I had no plan, no direction, and I was basically living life in a random fashion. Though I did learn a lot from that experience, I will state that I will never, ever live like that again. Basically, I label those five years of my life as the dark ages.

This chapter will focus on living your life intentionally. In the extremely successful movie Forest Gump, Forest's mother tells him that *"life is like a box of chocolates, you never know what you're going to get"*. As a matter of fact, at the very beginning of the movie, there was a white feather floating around the town center where Forrest was sitting and he randomly picks up the feather only because it unintentionally falls at his feet. The movie is roughly about a lovable man who by no plan of his own becomes a very wealthy man. Though I love the movie, I will say when comparing life to a box of chocolates, I would rather intentionally buy a big box of Turtles. Though the candy may come in slightly different shapes, at least I'll have an idea of what to expect and I can better prepare my taste buds for what I'm about to digest.

Having a plan is the best way to ensure that you are serving your purpose and keeping on track and achieving your goals. Being aware of your plan assists you in being aware of your surroundings and it increases your ability to properly react to circumstances and situations around you. It is very hard to forget the financial crisis of 2008. Though we are over a decade removed from that crisis, many of us still are almost anxious of a crisis of that magnitude happening once more. However, through all of the financial negativity during that period, there is one very valuable lesson in planning that I learned.

Looking Ahead

Back in 2006, Ford Motor Company mortgaged a good deal of its assets to secure over $25 billion in loans. During that same period, Ford sold off Aston Martin, Volvo, Jaguar, and Land Rover in order to focus more on improving their brand and preparing to navigate through a global economic crisis in which, in many aspects, the company foresaw on the horizon. Many economic experts at the time thought that Ford Motor Company's moves were not in line with the economic environment of 2006. At that time, the US and global economy was extremely stable and growing at a healthy pace. However, that growth would soon come to a screeching halt.

The economic slowdown of 2008, also known as the Great Recession, brought many large corporations to its knees. The automotive industry was affected severely so much in fact that both Chrysler and General Motors had to be bailed out and ultimately controlled by the United States government. Ford, on the other hand, planned and prepared for such a calamity. As a result of this preparation, Ford did not need assistance from the federal government.

The Ford story provides an excellent example of the need to plan ahead. Planning can never be done in a bubble. The experts who questioned Ford's decision to sell off assets and mortgage other assets were probably thinking in the short term. Ford was making decisions to pull back and build cash reserves at a time when the stock market was strong, the housing market was booming, and people were buying vehicles. So, to those who doubted Ford's decision may have determined that Ford was in a bad economic state. That was not the case at all. Ford realized that in the auto industry, things can always change. Ford recognized economic indicators that pointed to a major economic slowdown and decided to prepare themselves ahead of time.

When planning, you must think both internally and externally. Externally, you have to look to see what is changing around you. Those changes could be tangible and intangible. However the success of your plan depends on whether or not you recognize those external changes.

Equally important to recognizing what is changing, it is also important that you reasonably acknowledge tangible or intangible things that could change. For example, if you are making a career decision, it would be wise for you to thoroughly think out what is going on in the industry in which you will operate. Let's say for example you want to be a diesel engineer, and you apply at a premier engineering university. Before making that detailed commitment you should read about what's going on in the diesel industry. Then you need to determine if the time you are putting in getting an engineering degree focused on diesel power will benefit you in the long term. In this example, the person making this career decision must take into account the fact that engine companies like Cummins and others are spending a lot of money in research and development on large engines that are powered by other forms of energy. It is quite possible that being a diesel engineer may not be a career that will be in high demand for the super long term.

Also, when making a plan, it is important to make sure that your plan matches your purpose. Once I was talking to a student who wanted to become an underwater welder. However, he had planned to buy a home in Rosedale, Indiana. I then asked him if there were a lot of underwater welding opportunities in Rosedale Indiana. He paused for a moment and decided that maybe Rosedale Indiana is not a place for someone with the career of underwater welding. He revisited his plan and decided to buy a home in Gulf Shores Alabama. Planning a road trip across the country, it is imperative that your plan aligns with your destination.

Types of Planning

Primarily, there are two different types of planning. Those primary types of planning are strategic planning and tactical planning. Strategic planning is more proactive planning. It is what you originally set out to do. For example, I plan on writing my bike 20 miles on the trails today. However, just when you get ready to leave, it is pouring blinding rain that prevents you from riding your bike on the trails. So instead of writing your bike 20 miles on the trail, you place your bike on the bike trainer and *"ride"* for an hour and ½ inside. What you did instead was your plan *"B"*. That is an example of tactical planning or reactive planning.

We will get into a lot more detail of strategic planning in the next few chapters. I do want to share some examples of what strategic planning looks like before going into great detail. Though there are tons of horror stories in the airline industry, Southwest Airlines has represented the epitome of sound strategic planning. First, they have a purpose of being a low-cost no-frills airline. There are several low-cost no-frills airlines operating today, but few are known for customer satisfaction. Most of the people I talked to who use Southwest Airlines are relatively satisfied with their service. A lot of that satisfaction comes from their devotion to their purpose, and their meticulous strategic planning approach.

One way that Southwest Airlines effectively serves its purpose is through only using one type of aircraft, the Boeing 737, by doing that they do not have to worry about varied maintenance requirements. They only have to adhere to the requirements associated with the Boeing 737. Also, Southwest Airlines is very intentional about their flight destinations. This also helps in keeping costs down. Also, like in the Ford Motor Company example, Southwest Airlines thinks ahead. One thing Southwest Airlines does to keep costs down is they have been known to hedge fuel prices. Hedging is an investment practice that is primarily done when it comes to commodities. By hedging jet fuel, Southwest Airlines has been able to obtain a little more control over fuel costs than other airlines. This has surely helped Southwest Airlines in maintaining profitability.

Strategic planning is basically proactive planning designed in a way for you to achieve your purpose. Strategic planning is your *"to-do list"* of items that need to be accomplished in order for you to serve your purpose and achieve your goals. Proactive planning can be seen as the *"ideal"* plan. However, we all know not everything goes as planned, and sometimes, (most times), modifications to your plan must be made.

In some ways, these modifications are part of tactical planning. Tactical planning is more of a reactive type of planning. Though you don't always want to live in a tactical planning world, tactical planning is very important, and if done well it can lead to resounding success. All one has to do is look at the story of Bill and Scott Rasmussen.

Bill Rasmussen was the communications manager for the New England Whalers, a WHL hockey team which eventually became the Hartford Whalers, and ultimately the Carolina Hurricane. Rasmussen was fired from his job as the communications manager of the hockey team and shortly after teamed up with a man by the name of Ed Eagan and created the idea of having a cable television program focused on local sports in the Connecticut area. The idea of hosting local sports grew, and eventually, hockey, baseball, and college sports teams in the area began broadcasting their games on Rasmussen and Eagan's network. By September 1979, tens of thousands of viewers tuned in to watch what is now known as ESPN SportsCenter. Rasmussen went from a man who was determined to make a name for himself in professional hockey to a man who spread sports broadcasting throughout the world.

Rasmussen showed a willingness to change and modify his original strategic plan, and his tactical plan seemed to really work out well. Change in flexibility is essential in achieving your purpose and goals. You must never be married to your plan. Always remember that things around you are not static. They are constantly changing, and you must be willing and capable of making modifications to your plan while at the same time achieving your goals and serving your purpose. I'm not saying that you should be like the feather in the movie Forest Gump, but I am saying there are times you have to navigate life very much like Capt. Sully did when landing in the Hudson River. There are times that you have to be intentional when changing course. One of the best ways to be successful when changing course is to be strong enough to navigate during the winds of change.

One example of an organization staying married to their plan is Blockbuster Video. Blockbuster Video is probably the most successful movie video rental company ever. At its peak, it had well over a thousand stores and tens of millions of rental customers. The biggest mistake Blockbuster made was that it wasn't willing to change with the times.

Technology played a major role in the demise of Blockbuster. Movie rental companies like Netflix recognized that a change in the delivery of home movie rentals was coming. However, Blockbuster could not look past its success in the past. As a result, falling behind its customers while other rental service delivery methods to stay ahead of its customers. Blockbuster tried to react and was even acquired by Dish Network in 2013. However, all of Blockbuster's maneuvers were too little too late, and a once giant and popular organization became the epitome of 90s nostalgia and a lesson in poor business planning.

Though this provides a great business example, you must ask yourself how many times have you just stuck to the plan? It is imperative that as individuals we don't get stuck in the "that's how I always do it" mentality. We must all be cognizant of the change around us, and we must be ready and willing to navigate through the change.

If anything, this new decade has taught us that we are in a constant state of change seemingly more now than ever before. Simply go back and think about what you were doing in February 2020 and look at what you are doing now. Then, look at everything you endured in between. There was COVID, the summer 2020 protests and riots, the ever-contentious 2020 election and the chaos that came after. We are slowly getting back to *"normal"*. However, our normal now consists of supply chain shortages, worker shortages, and high inflation. Hopefully, you recognize these changes and have been able to modify your plan and purpose to adjust to our new reality.

Though my last paragraph is pessimistic, I implore you to not plan in a negative fashion. It is imperative that you always set your goals and plan positively. Always focus on how you can utilize the resources that are at your disposal. If you plan by focusing on what you don't have, chances are you won't move on your plan at all. Your purpose and goals are designed for positive success and satisfaction in your life, so it is important that you focus on the things that are at your disposal that will help you achieve that success. Though it is important to recognize the obstacles that can impede your success, it is equally important to positively utilize your resources to overcome those obstacles.

Chapter 8

Positive Planning

About 10 years ago, I was teaching a class at the Indianapolis campus of Ivy Tech Community College. It was a Saturday morning class, and it had a mixture of people from several different majors. I had a female student in that class that often arrived at the classroom before me. The class started at 8 AM, I usually arrived at the class at about 7:40 AM, and I was almost always certain that she would be there before me. Sometimes she would wait at the class door for me to unlock the room. Other times, if security saw her sitting there, they would let her in.

One Saturday I arrived at my usual time, and the student was not yet there. As a matter fact, we were 15 to 20 minutes into the class before the student arrived. When she arrived, she was not acting like herself, and she was wearing very dark sunglasses. She was very quiet, and did not engage in class discussion like she usually would. The Saturday class lasted three hours, and to my surprise she remained quiet for the duration of that class session.

After I dismissed class, that student sat at her desk and waited for everyone to leave. Because I had to lock the door, I waited for everyone to leave as well. It was then that she came up to me. She took off her glasses and showed me not one but two black eyes. The night before class, her boyfriend, jealous because she was attending school, beat her up. He did so in front of her daughter, and when she had the opportunity, she called 911 and had him arrested. Because the apartment that they lived in was his, she decided to take her daughter and move that night to an emergency shelter.

After hearing this horrible news, my automatic response was to assist her and give her extra time to get her assignments done. However, she did not ask for that. What she did need was a place to do her schoolwork, not only for my class but for her other courses. When she left her boyfriend's house, she also had to leave a computer behind because the computer was his and not hers. My classroom was a computer lab, and she wanted to stay after class on Saturdays for a few hours to get all of her assignments done. I had no problem accommodating her, and I notified security of the situation so they would not lock my door and lock her out of getting her assignments done in a timely manner.

For about three weeks, the student would stay after class, and I would instruct the student to make sure she notified security when she was done with the room. On Saturday, the student walked out when all the other students walked out of class when class was over. I remember looking at her and jokingly saying that I know you have at least one assignment to type up because I just gave you one. She smiled and said that over that past week she was able to find a computer and she also found an apartment that she could afford. With a look of satisfaction, she said that her and her daughter finally have a home.

Clearly, that student had a desire to fulfill her purpose and she was going to utilize every resource that she could to do so. Through her tragedy and misfortune, the student was able to focus on positive resources and positively plan on ways to achieve her goal. After she was no longer my student, we became friends on Facebook. As a faculty member I was able to attend her college graduation when she became a surgical tech. And through Facebook, I was able to be a witness to her buying a beautiful three bedroom home in Brownsburg, Indiana for her and her daughter. She is married now, and has two other children. Her positive planning yielded positive results.

Positive goals

One may say that all goals are positive. However, that is not necessarily the case. Some goals, if not set properly, can unintentionally deliver results that were not entirely desired. Take the story of my student. She was surrounded by negative circumstances and lack of resources. However, she focused on what was available to her. As a result, she was able to successfully achieve her goals.

Positive goal setting is a technique where you word your goals in a positive manner. Back in the late '90s, my father was very ill with cancer, and he decided that he was going to quit smoking.

That was his goal, *"quit smoking"*. My father was a very disciplined person, and he quit smoking after almost 50 years, cold turkey. However, he still did not exercise, he did not eat healthy, and he continued to drink hard alcohol. Though he did quit smoking, his other lifestyle choices caused him to live the final 20 years of his life in extremely bad health. When he died in 2013, he was suffering from diabetes, an extremely bad liver, and COPD.

If my father decided to set the goal of living a healthy lifestyle, he may have been able to live his final years with a better quality of life. If the goal were to live a healthy lifestyle, he would've not only quit smoking, but he would have committed to actions that led to a healthier way of life. It is quite possible that just by the simple wording of a goal, the outcome would have matched his intended desire. Instead, the final five years of his life created an unnecessary strain on him and those who cared for him.

When it comes to positive planning, think of it this way. Let's say you are like most people and have more debt than what you would like to have. Instead of setting a goal of getting out of debt, set a goal of being financially sound. If you set a goal of getting out of debt, you may achieve that goal. However, if you are not doing other financial exercises to prevent you from going back into debt, there is a good chance you will fall into debt once more. With that being said, a great way to set a financial goal is to plan on designing a financial lifestyle that will assist you in achieving your purpose. A financial goal may include building a formidable savings, paying cash and only using credit in emergency situations, and paying more than the minimum balance on credit cards and other secured and unsecured loans such as mortgages, personal loans, and car notes. By setting your goals in a positive manner, your habits will change in a way that will prevent you from falling back into an undesired circumstance.

Be MacGyver

Back in the late 80s and early 90s, was a television show that chronicled the life of a secret agent played by Richard Dean Anderson. The show was named MacGyver, and it was very successful for that period of time. Back in 2016, there was a reboot of the show with a different cast, but the show did not garner the level of success the original series enjoyed. In this show, MacGyver would find himself almost weekly in a difficult situation with very little resources at his disposal. However, he would utilize nonsensical resources to his advantage and happened to use those resources to successfully get out of his difficult situation. Back when the show was popular, my friends and I used to joke that MacGyver could use a gum wrapper and a paperclip to fly to the moon. Though most of the antics on the show MacGyver were extremely unrealistic, there is a lesson to be learned. That lesson is to focus on what you have and use them in an innovative fashion towards achieving your goals.

The original story provided at the beginning of this chapter about a woman who left an abusive relationship all while attending school is a perfect example of focusing on the tools that you do have. For example, when the student left the computer that she used to complete her homework, she didn't come to me and say that she didn't have a computer. She came to me and asked if she could have access to one of the computers that were in the computer lab. She went and looked at the classroom schedule and saw that there were no more Saturday classes after mine. I have a feeling that if I said no, that student would have found a computer that she could have used Saturdays after our class. That student did not focus on obstacles; she focused on opportunities.

Like MacGyver, think outside the box and be innovative with the tools in which you have access. I remember one time, a long time ago, the icemaker on my father's refrigerator broke. I was no longer living in my father's home, so this icemaker must've broken sometime after 1989. I was born in 1971, and that refrigerator was two or three years older than I was. My father was determined to make sure that this refrigerator outlived everyone in the house. He called Whirlpool in order to get replacement parts, but those replacement parts were made obsolete long ago. So instead of buying a new refrigerator, he tore the entire ice maker apart, and with nuts and bolts and fishing string, he fixed that icemaker.

My father moved out of that house in 2001, and that icemaker never broke down again. I often wonder if the people who bought the house after him used that refrigerator for a little while. It would be nice to know if someone still got some use from that old rust-colored refrigerator. Out of necessity, and determination, (I may want to add an insane level of frugalness), my father looked for resources that he did have in order to prevent him from buying a brand-new refrigerator.

One of the most valuable tools that is always at your disposal is experience. Both good and bad experiences are great tools to possess. Back in 2019, a well-known textbook publisher approached me to write a marketing textbook. I had always wanted to write a textbook, and I was delighted and excited for this opportunity. The content of the textbook, and I must admit, there is a lot of good stuff in that textbook. One big problem, not one college (including the colleges in which I taught), accepted the book for their curriculum. Not because it was poorly written, but because it did not fit their textbook distribution plans.

I started writing my textbook in 2019. Though it is true I could not anticipate that there was going to be a global pandemic that would have a significant impact on college classroom and the methods in which classes are held and course content is delivered, looking back I really could have anticipated that was a growing trend in colleges and universities utilizing open educational resources, (which are for the most part free resources to students), as opposed to using traditional, and pricey college textbooks. My book was completed in the summer of 2020, and by that time most of the schools that I worked with had already adopted the open educational resource model. The only way they would take my book as if it was offered as a free resource. After much negotiation between the publisher and the universities, it was best that that textbook was put on the shelf. As disappointing as my first venture in textbook writing went, I am more determined than ever that my next textbook will be a success and serve the purpose of educating traditional and nontraditional students in the fundamentals of business management and marketing.

Unfavorable experiences can be one of the greatest resources if not the greatest resource, you can have when creating a positive plan. Take my textbook experience for example, from those missteps I have learned some valuable lessons, and I will take those lessons and apply them to the new book I'm currently writing. Keep in mind, and not reviewing those unfavorable experiences negatively, I am viewing those experiences as a useful tool in planning for my next textbook.

My past experiences in textbook writing have taught me to be more mindful of the audience and the climate in which I am writing the textbook. Also, my past experiences taught me to make sure that I have the necessary partners working with me to make sure the textbook is successful. Also, the next textbook will have holistic consideration. Meaning, that by communicating with key partners, not only will I be focusing on the content of the book and the other aspects in order to successfully get the book to the college and university market. Yes, my first venture into the textbook industry was disappointing. However, I am looking forward to the potential success of my next venture into the textbook industry.

People who need People

Back in 1964, Barbra Streisand released a song titled, **People**. As a kid, I will admit that my friends and I used to make fun of some of the lyrics. Of course, growing up in the 80s when songs like Pac-Man Fever were successful hits, looking back, we had no room to make fun of Barbra Streisand. Now that I've grown up, there is one line of Streisand's song that should resonate with anyone creating plans, and that is *"people who need people are the luckiest people"*.

It is important to understand that one should never plan for their future in a bubble. You should always have mentors, advisors, and trusted family members to assist you in creating the plan necessary to achieve your goals and purpose. It is important to have mental investors and those are people that you can run ideas by to see how they react. These would be individuals that you trust, and they trust you enough to feel comfortable in offering constructive criticism and insight to those ideas and plans.

Also, you need emotional investors. Remember I told you that every morning on my way to work I would call my mother to see how she was doing and tell her about my day. My mother was more of a cheerleader to help me get motivated and ramped up for the trials and tribulations that most all of us experience in their place of employment. At the end of the day, I would call my father on my way home. My father was indeed not the cheerleader. He was very much a realist, and when talking to him in the evening, he would put my challenges and opportunities in a very realistic perspective. Those calls to my mother and father were extremely helpful due to the fact that I knew that both of them were emotionally invested in my success. My father has since passed, but his advice from my previous phone calls with him can still be replayed over and over again in my mind. My mother is still very much alive, and I still call her every day. Those calls are very valuable to me immensely in helping me navigate through life. If you do not call your parents every day, start. It is good for all of you.

In addition to mental investors and emotional investors, it is important that you have accountability partners. People who hold you accountable are extremely valuable. They are people who will help you keep on track. I remember when I finally decided to go and get my PhD. I told some very important people in my life about my decision. I didn't say it to brag, but I said it so that those individuals would occasionally ask me in conversation how my PhD journey was developing. I would hate to have told them that I quit, so those people were inadvertently my accountability partners.

You could also have partners that are intentional accountability partners. Many churches have prayer partners where they actually match up people and they hold themselves accountable when it comes to matters of faith. In areas of addiction recovery and the like, people are often assigned recovery coaches. Again, these are individuals who hold others accountable in their journey to recovery. Accountability partners are carrying people who help others maintain their discipline and achieve their goals and purpose. When it comes to people these individuals serve as a valuable resource.

Another important human resource would be having strategic partners. These are individuals who may already be at the destination in which you one day wish to arrive. These partners are your *"connections"*. These individuals may be retired individuals from the field you wish to enter, they may be trusted individuals in the community, political or religious leaders, or maybe just someone you've grown to trust.

Strategic partners can help you on your journey to success. They may *"know a guy"* that can help you obtain an interview. They also may be important in providing guidance in how to navigate a particular journey. Strategic partners are very important and can provide a boost to help you achieve your desired goals and purpose. However, you must be careful and not unintentionally make your relationship with strategic partners a one-way affair. If strategic partners and mentors feel that they are being used, those people may shy away from you. Always make sure that you have something to offer to your strategic partners.

Something as simple as genuine appreciation will make it so a strategic partner will become well-vested in your future success and will do anything they can to guide you on your journey.

In keeping with the essence of strategy, one of the most important and positive aspects to achieving your goals is to be strategic-minded. Strategic partners can help you in obtaining and maintaining a strategic mindset that is necessary to achieve your goal and purpose. Strategic partners can help you better recognize your future. They can guide you in trends, and they can provide valuable insight to your own inner being.

Being strategic-minded will allow you to be proactive as opposed to reactive. Just like the game of chess, strategy is anticipating what your potential moves in the environment around you. Strategy is not only internal, it is external. Having sound strategic partners is essential to positive planning.

Chapter 9

Planning with the Strategic Mindset

This chapter will provide step-by-step tips you are free to use when developing a plan to achieve your goals and purpose. These steps have been used effectively for organizations around the world. If personalized, the steps can assist in creating the ideal plan for your future. These steps can help in realistically setting your short-term, medium-term, and long-term goals.

Pepsi Co. planning

When I was working on my MBA at Anderson University in Indiana, my capstone class professor, Dr. Jeffrey Buck, gave the class a final assignment to analyze the strategic plan of Pepsi. The most important lesson that I learned from that exercise is the importance of proactive and intentional planning. In Pepsi's case, the company struggled to compete with the Coca-Cola company regarding having their soft drinks in fast-food restaurants. Pepsi purchased fast food chains and eventually created the company Llama Foods which consists of restaurants like Taco Bell, Kentucky Fried Chicken, A&W, and Long John Silver. Pepsi company is also the owner of the world's most popular sports drink Gatorade due to their purchase of Quaker foods. These were strategic moves designed for PepsiCo to remain the beverage powerhouse it is now.

Be proactive and intentional

The Oxford dictionary defines strategic as *"carefully designed or planned to serve a particular purpose or advantage"*. Making plans for your life, whether it be professional or personal, it is important that you do your very best to make sure that every move you make is by design and for your advantage. Though it is true you may not have that opportunity 100% of the time, it is important that you try to create that advantage the majority of the time. Living your life intentionally and with purpose is the very best way to find joy.

Your purpose statement

One of the most common items in all business plans is the mission or purpose statement. This statement verbalizes what an organization wants to achieve. For example, because I love playing hockey, one of my favorite companies is Bauer. At one time, Bauer's mission statement was *"To bring inspiration and innovation to every athlete in the world."*. With that statement in mind, every decision that Bauer makes when it comes to their hockey products revolves around innovation. Their products are used in abundance in every hockey league from Little League all the way up to the NHL.

When I was in the Navy recruiting school down in New Orleans, my instructor NCC Gary Leath introduced me to the 30-second *"elevator speech"*. According to Leath, the elevator speech was the sales pitch you would give someone if you were in an elevator. For example, if you are in an elevator with another individual, and that individual asks a question regarding who you are and what you do. An elevator speech response would be *"My name is Trunnis Goggins, and I am a business professor who works with many students around the country in order to help them obtain their undergraduate and graduate degree in business. I am also an author who writes self-help and textbooks. On the side, I am a business consultant and help young entrepreneurs in achieving and accomplishing their dreams of self-employment and individual accomplishment and success"*. Ideally, by the time you finish saying that statement, the elevator ride is over. However, that statement should have grabbed your audience's attention and maybe laid the groundwork for further conversation.

It is imperative when creating a plan that the first thing you do is create and establish your purpose. There must be a purpose behind your plan, so before you even start planning, you must have a firm idea of your purpose. Now, you should have multiple purposes. What I mean by that is you should have a personal purpose, a professional purpose, and a holistic purpose. Your holistic purpose is basically, without sounding morbid, what you would want someone to say about you at your eulogy. Your holistic purpose is your summation statement.

I know that most of you reading this book will find it very hard to balance your personal life and purpose with your professional life and purpose. However, with adequate planning you may be able to strategically devise a way to create more balance between your two lives. With the proper plan, you may be able to leverage your personal life to benefit your professional life and vice versa in a healthy way. By doing so, it is possible for you to achieve your holistic purpose.

Personal purpose statement

The most focused person I know is my son Noah. I do not think that he's ever written down a purpose statement per se. However, I do know that he wants to be a K-12 schoolteacher, and he is currently attending college to achieve that goal. When he was a senior in high school, I remember him telling me that he was going to take a year off from school so that he could decide what he wanted to do when it comes to careers. Many people worry that taking a year off of school will ultimately lead to two years of school, and then, (like me), lead to 17 years off of school before they finally buckle down and focus on college. That was not the case with Noah, he took a year to the day off from school and enrolled at Ivy Tech Community College with the plan of achieving his associates degree and then moving on to IUPUI in Indianapolis Indiana ultimately to achieve his teaching degree. That was his plan, and through discipline and hard work he has stuck to his plan.

Because he is determined to achieve his goal and purpose, he has adjusted his life accordingly to find the proper balance. Before college he was working full-time at a retail store, once he enrolled he requested to be reduced to part-time. He currently works every weekend and has a heavier schedule during college breaks. He also understands the need for downtime, and he makes sure he has time to attend Indiana Pacers games and occasionally go with me to watch my beloved Buffalo Sabers and Buffalo Bills. Though this may sound simple, I know that he has to work very hard to maintain this balance.

A personal purpose statement, once developed, can help you not only in creating a plan but in making day-to-day decisions. For example, let's say that you have a strong desire to be a good parent because you feel that your parents let you down in some way. Your purpose statement could read something like: *"I will strive to be the best parent I can be"*. Keep in mind that this purpose statement is only one sentence. This one sentence should now provide you with a guide for all future decisions.

For example, let's say that you are a single parent, and you meet someone at a party. The two of you hit it off in a conversation, and you decide to go out on a date. On that first date, you find out that this person you met at the party works part-time at a retail store, (which is an honorable position), but this person also sells recreational drugs on the side to supplement their income. This person wants to go out with you again. If you truly have bought into your purpose statement, you would absolutely know that going out with this person for a second date would not be conducive to being the best parent you can be. As a matter fact, developing any type of lasting relationship with this individual could bring undue harm to your child thus you failing both the child and your purpose. Example I gave you was very extreme, but illustrates how a purpose statement can assist in making sound decisions.

Professional purpose statements are also very valuable in helping you make wise career decisions. However, when it comes to career and professional purpose statements, one must be careful to not let money lead you astray. Take for example my story back in chapter one. My professional purpose statement contributes to my discipline. I was a business professor, and I absolutely loved teaching. As a matter of fact, I was in the middle of writing a very strong article on strategic planning that I was going to submit to an academic journal. I was derailed due to being offered a college administrative job that paid a considerable amount of money. The monetary enticement led me to move away from my purpose. Almost immediately, I did not feel right about my decision, and spent two full years feeling empty and professionally lifeless. I learned from that decision to always stay true to your purpose.

Finally, it is very beneficial if you have a holistic purpose statement. This is a statement that the person giving your eulogy would say about you at your funeral. For example, this statement could be something like *"Because of Betsy's compassion and ability to advise others, Betsy was able to mentor dozens of men and women in her community, and as a result, made her community a wonderful place to live"*. A holistic purpose statement is the statement that summarizes you in a nutshell. It is your lasting legacy. My maternal grandfather's name was Jack Gardner. He was a supporting husband, a loyal father, and a wonderful son to his mother. As a grandfather, Jack Gardner taught his three grandsons the benefit of hard work and the importance of saving money and getting a good education. However, for those who knew Jack Gardner in Brazil Indiana, he is remembered for his love of the United States military. As a matter of fact, he loved the military and his career in the military so much that his grandchildren affectionately called him *"Sgt. Jack"*. He died when I was 25 years old, and never in my life did I call him grandpa.

The United States Air Force and his decorated 30-year career was his legacy. He died in January 1996, and his funeral was one in which he was served full military honors. Ironically, right after his 21-gun salute, two F-16 fighter jets inadvertently flew over the cemetery. Though everyone at the graveside knew the jets were flying because of a training exercise, we all thought that maybe those pilots were flying over to salute their proud fallen Airman.

Look internally

When putting together a strategic plan, one of the most important things a company does is develop a SWOT analysis. SWOT stands for strengths, weaknesses, opportunities, and threats. Strengths and weaknesses are internally controlled, while opportunities and threats are external components that are largely outside of the control of the organization. In order to complete an accurate SWOT analysis, companies will conduct employee surveys, call in outside consultants, and have numerous board meetings in order to determine what their strengths, weaknesses, opportunities and threats are.

In almost all the previous chapters I mentioned self-reflection and self-analysis. When developing your personal SWOT analysis, self-reflection and self-analysis is extremely important, especially when analyzing and assessing your strengths and weaknesses. Fully determining your strengths and weaknesses, honest self-analysis, and conversations with trusted mentors and friends is very important.

Strengths

This is where self-reflection and self-analysis are extremely important. If self-analysis is not done correctly, it can lead to major disappointment and improper decision-making when it comes to deciding on goals and setting expectations. This is where you may either underestimate your true potential, or you may be overconfident in your desire and skill level. This miscalculation can lead to a great deal of regret and missed opportunities.

In the last chapter, I encouraged you to think about the resources that you do have at your disposal. Remember the story of the college student that got out of an abusive relationship, and how she effectively utilized the resources at her disposal in order to advance towards her ultimate goals? When deciding what your true strengths are, it is imperative that you do just that, look for strengths that you currently possess. For example, if you are trying to lose weight, do not focus on joining the gym in 30 days. Instead, focus on a set of dumbbells you have down in your basement. That is a resource that you have now. That is something that you can use now to actively work towards achieving your goals of weight loss and better health. If you focus on a potential gym membership in 30 days, you may delay your better health journey for that time period.

When it comes to long-term planning, you should always start out with a positive attitude. You should also plan with the present. Use your current resources as building blocks to obtain future resources. If you focus on resources that you don't have, the thought process may impede and interfere with you taking steps toward your goal. By taking a positive step towards planning, you can see the tools at your disposal that can help you achieve your goals and get you to your destination. However, you must also recognize that there are internal factors that can get in the way of achieving your goal. Those internal factors must be recognized and considered when developing your plan in achieving your purpose.

Weaknesses

Weaknesses are something that we all have but hate to recognize. Those weaknesses must always be considered when planning for your future. Weaknesses are always internal. When it comes to companies and organizations weaknesses can be financial, cultural, and operational. When it comes to individual weaknesses, those may include financial, mental/emotional, physical, and cultural. It is important to realistically recognize weaknesses. It is equally important to look at weaknesses in a positive light and not as a hindrance in goal accomplishment. By viewing your weaknesses in a positive light, you can leverage those weaknesses in your favor. In addition, by realistically recognizing your weaknesses, you can avoid making a decision that can put you in a vulnerable position.

Look externally

After deep self-reflection to consider internal factors that will influence and guide your decisions, it is important to look externally to determine how your environment may determine and guide your decision making. Every environment has opportunities and threats. Unlike strengths and weaknesses, opportunities and threats are items that you have very little to no control over. For example, let's say you want to be an elementary school teacher. Your strengths are that you are credentialed and qualified. Your weaknesses are you have an enormously soft heart for little children and in many ways, you spoil them. However, you can leverage that weakness in a way that will bring out the absolute best in students.

Externally, you live in a community where there are two elementary schools, and only three vacant elementary school teaching positions available. The opportunity is that there are three positions open. The threat may be that there are 100 people that are applying for those three positions. This external situation can most definitely affect your decision. The first is you apply for the position and are accepted. The second is you recognize that there are applicants that have applied for these positions and are more qualified than you are, so you look for other elementary school jobs. The third decision is you look at the skills you have and transfer those skills to another profession and stay in your community.

Opportunities and threats must always be considered in your decision-making process. Regardless of the advantages you have internally, external forces provide a major influence and sometimes hindrance on achieving goals and your purpose. Depending on the circumstance, sometimes external elements may cause a person to alter their way of life in order to fully realize their purpose and potential.

Where there's a will

Back in 2019, at the esteemed opportunity to meet Anthony **"Champ"** Kelly. The reason behind our meeting was that one of his nonprofit football camp staff members invited me to volunteer and some of the young camp members about staying off the streets and staying in school. I found this to be a wonderful opportunity and accepted the invitation. When I arrived at the hotel the night before campus to start, I finally got to meet Champ in person. He and his wife greeted me as though they had known me for life, and I was part of their family. I felt very welcome.

In addition to running a nonprofit organization, Champ Kelly is the current Assistant General Manager of the Las Vegas Raiders. This individual has a deep passion for football, and when I was volunteering at his football camp, I remember him telling the kids there's more to the NFL than just being a player. Immediately after he told those young campers that, he then told the kids that he worked for the NFL, but he was not a player.

Champ and I communicate often, but I have never asked him what his purpose statement was. He may not even have a purpose statement. However, if he did, I am sure it was to make a positive contribution to the game of football. And that is something that he surely is doing. Not only at the professional level, but he has used the game of football to influence the lives of many children. At his football camps, there are several people involved in the NFL, including players. For those kids to be on the field with players that they look up to is surely going to have a lasting and positive effect on their lives.

Like so many athletes, I am confident that Champ wanted to be a part of the NFL from a young age. He had an outstanding high school career which led them to play collegiate football for Kentucky. He did not make it to the NFL as a player, but he did play professionally for the United Indoor Football (UIF) league. Champ recognized his strengths, weaknesses, opportunities and threats, and made sure he went on and got his MBA. His knowledge for football and business eventually got him an administrative job for the Lexington Horsemen. That experience in the UIF eventually led to him getting a scouting job for the Denver Broncos which led to becoming the director of scouting for the Chicago Bears and ultimately his current position in Las Vegas.

Champ Kelly, through strategic planning and perseverance, realized his dream to be a part of the NFL. I hope one day Champ gets a Super Bowl ring, (I also strongly hope that is after the Buffalo Bills gets theirs). There is no one that I know that as mortars of such an honor. His professional life story is a prime example of how realistic and strategic planning can help you realize your goal. His story is an inspiration to many on sound strategic planning in both a professional and personal sense.

There's a Will: The Journey of Champ Kelly

Since the original publication of this book in March 2024, Champ Kelly has undergone a remarkable professional journey filled with both opportunities and challenges. Once serving as the assistant general manager of the Las Vegas Raiders, Kelly stepped into the role of interim general manager following the termination of the previous GM. This shift placed him at the forefront of one of the NFL's most scrutinized organizations.

During his interim leadership, the Raiders' coaching staff, players, and fans began to witness a notable cultural transformation. While the team's record during his tenure was not enough to turn the season around, there was a clear and growing sense of optimism. Many believed that Kelly possessed the vision, temperament, and football intellect necessary to lead the Raiders into a brighter future. Despite the glimmers of promise and the foundational changes he helped initiate, the Raiders' ownership decided to move in a different direction for the 2024 season.

In a decision that surprised many—including myself—Champ was not retained as the full-time general manager. However, in a testament to his humility and professionalism, he agreed to continue serving as the assistant GM. At the conclusion of the 2024 season, Champ Kelly and the Las Vegas Raiders amicably parted ways. I vividly remember the moment I learned of this development. As someone who deeply respects Kelly's dedication and talent, I was genuinely disheartened. I knew that had he been given a fair chance, the outcome for the team could have been drastically different.

Despite the disappointment, I remain confident that Kelly's time will come. His unwavering will to succeed, his deep passion for the game of football, and his natural leadership ability will eventually lead him to a permanent general manager role. During his brief tenure in Las Vegas, these qualities were evident to anyone paying attention—from the locker room to the fans in the stands.

THE 4P'S OF YOU

Currently, Champ Kelly has taken on a new role as the senior personnel executive for the Miami Dolphins. Yes, for those who know me, that means he's now operating within the same division as my beloved Buffalo Bills. In good humor and loyalty to my team, I remember texting him my well wishes—for success in 15 of the 17 regular season games. He responded with grace and understanding, knowing my diehard allegiance to Buffalo.

Champ's drive is only strengthened by the support system he has around him. His family, especially his wife, plays a pivotal role in his journey. She stands beside him, not only as a partner but also as a planner, motivator, and believer in his vision. Their shared commitment to excellence in the world of professional football is truly inspiring.

There's a reason I say *'There's a Will."* Because when you have the will, you find a way—even when plans change, opportunities are delayed, and doors close unexpectedly. A strong will allows a person to face adversity and still maintain forward momentum toward their purpose. Champ Kelly embodies this principle completely.

As I wrote in the first edition of this book, I continue to believe that Champ Kelly will become a champion in the world of professional football. His journey is not just a story of a man working in sports—it's a lesson in perseverance, adaptability, and vision. And most importantly, it's a reminder that when there's a will, there's always a way.

Be strategic in your goals

It is a New Year tradition for people to come up with resolutions. One of the principal jokes in the fitness world is that the busiest day at the gym is January 2. That is primarily because so many people make New Year's resolutions to lose weight and become physically fit in the new year. Usually by January 31, it becomes much easier to find a parking spot at the gym of your choice. That is because for many, New Year's resolutions are not specific and not planned properly. I always tell people instead of having resolutions, you should always have a goal.

I got out of the Navy in May 2008, and when I left I weighed 177 pounds. Like many veterans, once they leave the service, they continue to eat the same but they tend to exercise less. As a result of this behavior, I really started to gain weight. One day in 2011, I got on the scale and weighed over 200 pounds. For someone of my height, that was unacceptable. Since it was close to the holidays, I decided to not start my exercise and weight loss plan until January 1. However, I refused to call it a resolution. Instead, I called it a maintenance plan.

Between the time I decided to start this journey and January 1 of 2012, I started doing research on the best way to get back to my desired weight. I started researching exercise plans and food plans. Also, I was realistic. I knew that I loved eating sweets, so I knew I was not going to give those up. As a result, I had to alter my exercise in a way to make sure I can still get to my desired weight while still eating basically what I wanted. That meant that exercising three days a week as recommended was not going to cut it and I had to exercise more.

Another thing I did back in 2012 was create a spreadsheet that tracked my exercises and the time I exercised. It also tracked my weight at the beginning and end of each week. I still use that spreadsheet to this day. I remember entering my first weight was 201 pounds. I really do hope I never see that again. I weigh in daily, and I usually weigh anywhere between 175 pounds and 180 pounds.

Through all of my research on this new lifestyle I was going to lead, I found that losing a large amount of weight at one time can be dangerous. Also, the chances of gaining that weight and then some back were relatively high, so I decided to break my weight loss down in 10-pound increments. My initial goal was to go from 201 pounds to 185 pounds by the end of 2012. That was my ultimate long-term goal for that year. In order to effectively track that I broke that 15 pounds down into 12 short-term goals of a net loss of 1.5 pounds a month. So that meant at the beginning of January when I weighed 201 pounds, I achieved my short-term goal if I weighed 199.5 pounds on January 31. I actually did achieve that and then some because I finished that month off at 197 pounds. That short-term goal gave me a sense of accomplishment and motivated me to complete the ultimate goal of 185.

When setting goals it is important to not try to eat the entire elephant in one bite. It is imperative that you achieve your ultimate goal one step at a time. That means setting short-term goals which are any goals less than 30 days. Short-term goals should build to midterm goals which are anything from 31 days to six months. A combination of the short-term and midterm goals will ultimately lead to your long-term goal which is six months to a year or more.

With my maintenance plan, my ultimate goal was to get back to 177 pounds and maintain that weight for the duration. I did hit that weight in 2015, and I've maintained the desired weight range since that time. I attribute my success to being realistic, implementing and maintaining a regiment of exercise, and making adjustments to my regiment when I fall outside of my desired weight range. Again, my ultimate goal was achieved by setting short, medium, and long-range goals. However, there was a time when not having a follow-up goal led to an undesired result.

Like so many college students today, I was a nontraditional student. I had flunked out of school my first time back in 1990 at Buffalo State. And I did not return to college until 2004 when I was 33 years old. I attended Marian University in Indianapolis Indiana, and I truly enjoyed that experience. I enjoyed it so much that I decided to move on to get my MBA. At the time, Marian did not have an MBA program, so I applied and was accepted to Anderson University in Anderson Indiana. My ultimate goal was to get my MBA, leave the Navy, and get a finance job back in my home state of New York. That plan changed because around the time I was close to completing my MBA, the great recession of 2008/2009 was occurring. I decided then to alter my career path and decided to get into higher education to teach business. I applied and was accepted to Walden University where ultimately received my PhD in public policy and administration with a major in nonprofit management.

For almost 12 years, I was operating in an environment where it was imperative to have structured goals. Short-term goals obviously were weekly homework assignments and tests, medium-term goals were getting good grades in semesters, the long-term goal was obtaining my degrees. Also during that time, my professional goals were structured in higher education due to the fact that my promotions were directly tied to my academic accomplishments. I did have an immediate goal after achieving my PhD of becoming a department chair, and I achieved that goal at Ivy Tech Community College in Indiana. However, somewhere immediately after achieving my PhD, I lost the art of articulating my own goals. As a result, I fell into a professional funk while I was still being promoted. I got to the point I was following someone else's plan and not my own.

I shared that story because I cannot stress enough the importance of always planning and setting goals. Make sure that every goal that you plan is a stepping stone to another goal or plan. We often hear of people dying shortly after they retire. I mainly attribute that to individuals who just stop planning and setting goals. My mother recently retired, and she has now started hiking, goes on hiking trips, and is setting goals to hike in various places. She is acting upon those goals by training multiple days a week. In addition, I had the opportunity of meeting a person who is 99 years old and was the physical fitness director at his assisted living facility. I asked him what keeps him going, and he said *"he always looks forward to tomorrow, and that day he stops looking forward to the next day my life will be finished"*. That was one of the most poignant pieces of advice I've ever received.

Evaluate and measure

Setting goals and planning requires constant evaluation and measurement. Just like when I was on my weight loss journey to live a healthier life, I built the spreadsheet. I wanted to know every single day my exact weight. I wanted to evaluate what I was doing that was right, and what I was doing that was a waste of time. I also talk to other people who are either trying to live a healthier lifestyle, or those who are experts in living that healthy lifestyle. I wanted their input on what to do to achieve my goal. Even now, I'm still doing research in order to implement new exercise routines and supplement diet routines that will help me in maintaining my weight, and improving my overall athletic performance.

It is important to understand that the world is constantly changing, and the goal that you set out to do as little as six months ago may be irrelevant now. Hypothetically, think about an entrepreneur back in March 2020. He may see an opportunity to build a mask business with many different designs to protect individuals from COVID-19. In March 2020, masks were all the rage, and even companies like Louis Vuitton and Gucci were making facemasks. However, mask sales are down. Though the entrepreneur may still want to start a startup company, selling facemasks may not be a good product to put as her primary focus. Constant goal evaluation is important to the ultimate success of achieving your purpose.

Paint a picture

In the Adam Sandler movie **Waterboy**, Henry Winkler's character Coach Klein would always tell Adam Sandler's character Bobby Boucher to *"visualize and attack"* before he got on the football field. This strategy allowed Boucher to make spectacular tackles, and ultimately help his team win a collegiate championship. When setting your goals, visualizing and attacking your plan should always be a part of your strategy. I eventually want to have a 45-foot cabin cruiser, and every so often, I am on the Internet *"shopping"* for my ultimate retirement gift. This is clearly a long-term goal, but I am constantly visualizing the reality of having such a vessel.

In your goal setting, always make sure you are preparing yourself for your ultimate accomplishment. Remember, if planned realistically, your goals and desires are not a pipe dream. Through hard work and determination, they can be achieved. Along with hard work and determination, it is important that you have passion and persistence.

Chapter 10

The Right Team to Execute Your Game Plan

The right team to execute your game plan, you will hear this more than once in this book, and that is you cannot achieve purpose solely on your own. You absolutely need people around you to help. You need to network and find the right people who are capable of helping you achieve your purpose. You must be interdependent. Dependent people cannot achieve their purpose because they are relying on others to achieve their dreams for them. Independent people always fall short of their ultimate purpose because they're doing everything on their own.

It is impossible to do everything on your own. People who micromanage always seem to run out of time or fall short in achieving their ultimate goal that is because they are trying to do absolutely everything. It is important that you find people who are willing to help you at the same time you're willing to help them. Every single team has multiple purposes. For example. In football, there are players out there who just want to make big money. They're going for the big contract and will possibly sacrifice the ultimate goal of the championship to achieve the ultimate payday. However, with that being said there are people on their team that have the goal of solely winning the championship.

Back in the early 2000s, both Brady and Peyton Manning were willing to take pay cuts in order to have the money available to sign players that were capable of giving them a championship. In both Peyton Manning and Tom Brady's cases, they did achieve their ultimate goal of obtaining a Super Bowl ring. So, it is not entirely out of the question for there to be different purposes yet striving for the same ultimate goal. If a team is willing to win a championship, they are probably willing to spend the money to obtain the right players to win a championship so again those goals do fit.

Throughout history, the most impactful leaders and innovators have all relied on a core group of individuals who enhanced their strengths and compensated for their weaknesses. Purpose, while personal, is never fulfilled in isolation. It is amplified in community.

This example is valuable in achieving your own purpose. It is imperative that you have the right people on your team. I remember when I first released the book *The 4P's of You*, I thought I had assembled the greatest team. My philosophy was the more money you spend the better return you get when it comes to team members. I remember putting a lot of money in the book itself. I remember my very first publisher of this book. Though they are a reputable publishing company and they do a great deal of good work, they were not the publishing company that really fit the goals and purpose of the book.

THE 4P'S OF YOU

As a result, the initial release of this book did not hit the market that I necessarily wanted to hit in the beginning. It caused a lot of setbacks in the release. The lesson I learned from this instance was to make sure that purposes though they may be different between one organization or one teammate to the next can align to achieve a similar goal. If you are finding people just because they serve a purpose and serve and satisfy a skill, you may run into a problem because the ultimate goal to be reached may not be entirely similar. Those differences can cause conflict and can also prevent one or even both team members from not achieving their desired goal

The same could be said with finding team members who are there to enrich themselves as much as enriching you. I've had many situations during this process in which there were people who did enrich themselves. There were a lot of people who made a lot of good money off of this book. Unfortunately, the *lot of good money* was not by me. They were involved in enriching themselves. They were not really oriented in the end mutual enrichment of myself. Often times I saw that when you would say social media posts by certain team members they would promote some things but they wouldn't promote the things that you asked them and begged them to promote also in times of return phone calls and things like that people did not do that on time as a result things were delayed or not even mentioned.

Also, people who are only on a team to enrich themselves are very poor listeners. Your goals are not as important to them as their goals are as a result communication even basic listening and directions are overlooked because it doesn't matter to that person. It is important that people on your team though they may share a different passion are passionate about the ultimate success of your mission and purpose. Yes, I am sure that those individuals want to succeed in their own right and they have their own personal missions, but your purpose in the accomplishment of your purpose must be important to them in achieving their purpose in building their reputation. It is imperative that there is some type of mutual benefit for both people being on a team.

Another thing I learned there are people who want to be on your team and care to be on your team but may not know how to achieve exactly the purpose you want to achieve. There are a lot of people who really do believe that they can help you in achieving your goal but may not have the exact capability to achieve their goal and your goal as a result. That leads to unnecessary failure or delayed success. It is imperative that anyone on your team be capable of whatever task they are willing to do regardless of how passionate they are to help you in achieving your goal.

When building a team you need to make sure that everybody has a clear vision of what you want to accomplish. You have a clear vision of what your team members want to accomplish once that is established the chances of building a successful team can be put in place. There are certain members that you need on your team. You need people that are on your team that are good at what you are not good at doing. For example, my team of building the 4P franchise would not be as successful if it wasn't for the versatile yet detail-oriented Nichol Perricci. Going back to the section of purpose, she is someone who keeps everything in check. I am the type of person that I have tons of ideas, and I want to throw them out there and get them out there as soon as possible. Yet Nichol has been instrumental in making sure that all details are in order. She does an excellent job of keeping everything in perspective. True success is found after finding someone of her magnitude.

Another teammate that you should have is someone who absolutely 100% believes in your mission. Dana Garrett is my life partner, yet just because she is my life partner does not mean that there is 100% belief. However, I do have that in Dana. By having someone like that on your team it gives you the confidence that is necessary to take risk and do things to be successful. That is because you know that any challenge presented you know that you have someone who has your back entirely. Since the beginning of this new journey, Dana has always had my back.

It is imperative that you have someone on your team who holds you accountable. I definitely have that in my dear friend on the other side of the world Jo Jackson. Jo is a coach, entrepreneur, and CrossFit athlete from Sydney Australia. She is a major fan of my brother's and a dear friend to me. We connected due to her movement called **The Dangerous Modern Man**. It is a fantastic movement you definitely have to pull that up for yourself.

She is the type of individual who motivates others and definitely tries to get the most out of others. That is probably why she is such a phenomenal coach professionally. When I was in Sydney recently, we were supposed to go and have drinks. She told me to meet her at some theater which I did. At this theater, there was a CrossFit competition named Turf Games. This was the first time I was ever in such an environment; I love competition and without a doubt I fell in love with CrossFit.

While there she convinced me that next year which is coming up I will be competing in a competition with her and others. I absolutely accepted the challenge. From that point when I came back to America, she has set weekly meetings with me and has worked with me to make sure that I am on course not necessarily to win the competition but to finish the competition successfully. She holds me accountable as far as what I eat, how I exercise, where I exercise, and she always has benchmarks for me to meet. Everyone needs a teammate and friend who is like Ms. Jackson and holds you accountable. This could be the coaching in her, but I really seriously believe that she is deeply concerned about my success. I absolutely appreciate that type of teammate and friend.

Finally, you do not have to like your teammates. Just because you like them doesn't make them a good teammate. I will and have discussed my time on the Chancellor's cabinet for Ivy Tech Community College Columbus Indiana. I will discuss and have discussed that as a team; they warrant many lasting friendships.

As a matter of fact, I never had any type of encounter with any of those members on that team outside of a professional setting. Even further, people when they left the team while I was there never even had a going away lunch or anything like that. They just simply left. Even in my case when I left after being on the campus for well over six years, the cabinet never offered a goodbye lunch or anything. Quite frankly, I'm really glad they didn't because it would've been uncomfortable saying goodbye when the salutations of "we're going to miss you" and things like that were not sincere. It was best just to walk away and leave. However, with all of that being said, many, many goals were achieved with that team. Though there wasn't any type of personal relationship to speak of between the members, professionally, the team worked well. In a similar situation, I would be honored to work with the team of that dynamic again. Emotional bonds can enhance morale, but professional respect and functional execution often matter more in delivering results. Cohesion is built through clarity of purpose, not just compatibility of personality.

On the same note, I have been on teams where people absolutely loved each other and yet nothing got done. I often think of my beloved Buffalo Sabres. How they always talk about how this is a family environment and this team has this type of culture and that type of culture and it's always loving and we all love each other and all that stuff. However, they have not been to the playoffs in well over a decade. Sometimes I wish they didn't like each other so much. Maybe the inner conflict would drive them to success. There are lots of times when teams do like each other so much. They focus on the relationships and not on results. As a result, purpose and goals are not necessarily achieved.

In building the 4P's franchise, I have realized the importance of creating and maintaining a strong team. Sometimes that means picking up new members while letting other members go. It is a part of the process. It is not to be taken personally. It is to be taken professionally. Sometimes there are great fits. Sometimes there are not. You have to be mindful of the direction your team is going at all times. If not you can come off track quite quickly. Sometimes you could be off-track for a long time and the chances of getting back on track in a timely manner are difficult at best.

So, to close out this chapter. It is important to have a strong team. It is equally important to always monitor the strengths and weaknesses, opportunities, and threats of your team. Without it. You may fall behind quickly.

Chapter 11

Passion

Back in the early 80s, Rod Stewart released a song titled Passion. Towards the very end of song, Rod Stewart sung these lyrics:

> *"You need passion, we need passion/can't live without passion/ Even the president needs passion/everybody I know needs some passion/some people die and kill for passion/nobody admits they need passion/some people are scared of passion/yeah, passion"*

Though not one of Stewart's more popular songs, the song does ring true. Everybody needs passion. Without passion, your plan and your purpose are almost destined to never be achieved.

One of the most passionate people I ever had the opportunity to meet was a pastor of the church I used to attend back in Indianapolis, Indiana. The church's name was Calvary Temple, it later changed its name to Caring Place and the pastor's name was Philip Meade. Pastor Meade was the assistant pastor of Calvary Temple for a number of years. You can tell by the way people interact with him that he has touched so many people's lives. He had a deep passion for the church and the congregation. During one of the most difficult times in the church's history, Pastor Meade stepped up to become the interim lead pastor, and his leadership and love prevented the church from breaking apart.

Pastor Meade worked very hard in the selection of his successor, and served as his successor's assistant pastor and mentor until he retired. After his retirement, his devotion to both the Lord and people compelled him to serve others. Pastor Meade's passion for service still lives on today at Caring Place church and is seen in various programs and outreach ministries serving Indianapolis, Indiana. Even I sought his counsel during a difficult time in my life, and through his passion I am able to share some of the things that I learned from him in this book.

Sustained Passion

Sustained passion leads to joy. According to the Merriam-Webster dictionary, the first definition of joy is *"the emotion invoked by well-being, success or by the prospect of possessing what one desires"*. If you look at the very beginning of the definition it speaks of *"well-being success"*. Well-being is a long-term situation. Many people, including the writer of the Declaration of Independence Thomas Jefferson, confuse joy with happiness. As a result, millions of people are pursuing happiness when in essence they should be pursuing joy.

Happiness is defined by the Merriam-Webster dictionary as *"pleasurable or satisfying experience"* or *"state of being happy"*. Just like I focused on well-being in the first definition of joy, let's focus on two words in the definition of happiness which are experience, and state. If you think about it, experiences and states fluctuate constantly. Think about how many times your state of mind and mood changes in a day. This confusion between joy which is constant and happiness which is fleeting can lead to inaccurate planning and poor decision-making.

I am confident that you can remember a time when you had a conversation with a friend or relative, and that friend or relative was venting about leaving their spouse or partner since that person no longer makes them happy. What may be true at that moment, is that person does not experience happiness with their partner. One question that you should always ask the person you are consulting or consoling is *"But do you feel joy?"*. There have been several relationships that have ended in regret because the question between joy and happiness was answered only after the relationship ended.

Sustained passion is essential to you achieving your purpose. Professionally, my passion in education is more about working directly with students, and far less about administration. While serving as an administrator at Ivy Tech Community College, I remember getting an opportunity to once again get back into the *"classroom"*. I had the opportunity to teach inmates because of a partnership between the Indiana Department of Corrections and our school. For the inaugural class of this partnership, my boss, who was the Chancellor of the Ivy Tech Community College Columbus campus attended my class as a guest speaker. He sat around and listened to a little bit of my lecture. Later on, he commented to me that I "was in my element" referring to the classroom. He went on to state that he had not seen me that excited in a while. My response to him was that it was what I loved.

I remember preparing for this course with great detail. My assistant at the time was phenomenal at getting me the resources I needed. As a result of this preparation, the inmates that were part of this program passed successfully. Though I am no longer an administrator at Ivy Tech, and as a matter of fact I no longer live in the state of Indiana. I will always be a part of this program because it is an element of my professional purpose.

In the professional environment, there are times when your professional purpose outlasts your legitimate role at an organization. We all know people who *"retire"* from a professional role only to come back to their organization to serve in a new role as a mentor or counselor. These people are extremely valuable to the future of their organizations and often time the future of their profession.

Personally, sustained passion in your purpose may outlive your very existence. I think about my dad's father who died back in 1985. All these years later, his influence still is visible in multiple generations of his family. His purpose was to make his family successful and Godly. Many of his descendants have gone on to become successful in business, educators, dentists, doctors, and lawyers. Also, there are several of my family who went into the ministry following in Douglas Goggins Sr's footsteps.

His purpose to raise his family out of poverty and segregation continued with my father. Now I know there are some of you who have already read about my father before reading this book. Some of you have a very strong opinion, and this book is in no way written to change that opinion. That being said, I must say that my father did a fantastic job in making sure that not only did my siblings and I not live in poverty, but all of us went on to become very successful individuals in our own right. That success even carried over to my children and my nieces and nephews. Whether my siblings and I like it or not, our father's words and philosophy, (though modified), are still spoken and practiced in our own households. My father's passion for success, not only his own but his children's success, became an obsession. My father's not here to defend himself, I will not present in this book the reasons that led me to believe in his obsession. However, I will talk about how obsession can negatively influence your true purpose.

Balancing obsession and passion

I've said it several times in this chapter, and it's warranted to say it once more. Sustained passion leads to joy. However, irrational passion leads to obsession. Obsession can lead to irrational decisions that can sabotage your true purpose. I love hockey and football. I will play and watch hockey at any chance I get, and if the Buffalo Bills are on TV you can bet your next month's mortgage payment that I will be watching. Though I am passionate about those sports, I keep their winning and losing in perspective. There are some sports fans that are obsessed with their team. I remember years back reading about a Pittsburgh Steelers fan who actually had a heart attack and died because he was watching and got too invested in a Steelers game.

Obsession is dangerous and some of the most compelling and disturbing true crime stories are rooted in obsession. One crime story in particular that still troubles me is the story of a woman who found out her husband was having an affair, and her obsession to save her marriage caused her to go to great lengths to look like the woman in which her husband was having the affair. She begged her husband to break off the affair and when that did not work, she followed her husband and his mistress to a hotel parking lot and there she took her car and hit her husband multiple times killing him. After her crime, she expressed a great deal of regret and was ashamed of her irrational decision because of the consequences that not only she suffered but her entire family.

There are numerous stories of celebrities who are obsessed with their appearance trying to maintain the appearance that made them so popular. Unfortunately, sometimes those great lengths to maintain an unnatural appearance led to death. There are also stories of successful financiers and businesspeople who are obsessed with success all the way to the point willing to defraud the elderly and those that trust them in order to maintain the appearance of success. It is imperative that you have passion. It is also imperative that you are mindful of that passion and can keep that passion rational and balanced.

A plan without passion is just a fantasy

Back when I was working on my PhD dissertation which focused on the strategic planning practices of nonprofit organizations, I conducted an interview with the senior vice president of an organization that provided various services to individuals with Down syndrome and those on the autism spectrum. We were discussing the strategic planning practices of this organization. This individual discussed the process in great detail, but then this individual said that after the process is done and the plan is approved, they put the strategic plan on the shelf and only bring it out when leadership wants to review it. This individual stated that they rarely if ever promote the plan to the subordinates in their department. My response to this was: how do you know if this plan is working, and how does the lack of commitment to the execution of the strategic plan affect other departments? This individual's reply was, *"It hasn't negatively affected the organization yet"*. This individual is right at that moment, the organization was doing quite well. However, just two short years after our conversation, another company took over that organization, and that individual was out of a job.

If you take time to create a plan, whether it be professional or personal, you must have a level of commitment and passion directed toward completing that plan. If that passion and commitment are not there, you might get lucky and successfully complete the plan. However, more than likely, you will fall victim to someone else's plan. Passion and commitment to a plan will compel you to always review your steps and measure your plan's successes and failures. Passion to your plan and its success will also create a mindfulness to recognize when and if modifications are needed in order to achieve your purpose.

When Bill Clinton was elected president in 1992, he had a very progressive agenda for that time. He proposed volunteer policies that would pay off college debt for individuals in public service. He also was the first president of the United States to present the idea of universal healthcare. In 1994 during the congressional elections, the United States sent a more conservative message to the White House. As a result, Clinton and his administration listened to the American public and proposed policies that would eventually lead to a balanced budget and less federal government intervention. As a matter of fact, one of Bill Clinton's famous quotes is *"The era of big government is over"*. Since Clinton was a child, his purpose was to become president of the United States. Clearly, he wanted to be known as a good president, and in order to do that he showed a willingness to modify his plan to better serve the American people. Today, people on both sides of the aisle recognize his accomplishments and contributions to the United States.

THE 4P'S OF YOU

Believe in yourself

Passion and belief in one's plan must also be accompanied by passion and belief in one's self. If you do not believe that you have the skill, resources, or discipline to successfully execute and complete your plan, there is virtually no chance that that plan will be accomplished. Without that plan accomplishment, your purpose will never be realized.

When I was the assistant recruiter in charge at a Navy recruiting station back in Indianapolis, we had a brand-new recruiter come on board. For the first two months, this recruiter struggled mightily in recruiting young men and women into the Navy. He made several mistakes and even tried to recruit people who were physically, legally, or mentally disqualified from enlisting in the military. His first month as a recruiter, he did not enlist one individual. The recruiter in charge and I were growing concerned. However, this sailor kept trying, and in his second month of recruiting, he finally got his first enlistment. After his first enlistment raised their right hand and signed the enlistment paperwork, the recruiter looked at the recruiter in charge and me and said, *"believe in yourself"*. The recruiter in charge and I looked at each other and rolled our eyes. This recruiter on the other hand became one of the superstar recruiters of Navy Recruiting District Michigan. His success in military recruiting continued long after the recruiter in charge and I left the recruiting station. I contribute the foundation to his success in his belief in himself.

Belief in oneself builds confidence. Confidence is essential in carrying out your plan. Healthy confidence also contributes to the passion needed to complete your purpose. Amazing what one can do when they are confident in themselves. However, it is imperative to not be overconfident because that can lead to not being successful in your plan in achieving your purpose.

One of the great examples of overconfidence is the story of the tortoise and the hare. We all know the story about how the hare was confident that he was faster than the tortoise, and did not take his race with the tortoise seriously. Tortoise on the other hand was determined to win the race, and through hard work and a steady pace, the tortoise was victorious.

I'm sure that there are numerous examples that we can draw off in modern times when it comes to overconfidence. In business, we can draw off the overconfidence that Blockbuster had when Netflix entered the video rental market. In US politics, in almost every election cycle, there is a story of a front-running candidate who was confident in victory only to get up the next morning and have to give their concession speech. Overconfidence is extremely prevalent in sporting events when an underdog absolutely manhandles the heavily favored opponent (being a Bills fan I've seen that one too many times over the past few years).

Like everything, believing in yourself and confidence must be properly balanced. Balance must be measured by you. There are those who look at you and your confidence and believe that you

THE 4P'S OF YOU

are arrogant. It may not be the case. For example, look at Mohammed Ali. Back in his prime, he was known for some stellar, and often hilarious trash talk. There are those back then who thought that he was very arrogant. However, even some of the greatest boxers of the modern era still consider Ali the greatest boxer of all time. It comes to believing in yourself, focusing on yourself and not the belief of others. Remember there are those that don't believe in you that you may not want believing in you at all.

Chapter 12

Passion and People

In the last chapter, I shared the importance of believing in yourself. I shared that belief in yourself fuels passion. Believing in yourself also can cause others to believe in you as well. However, never try to get everyone to believe you because not everyone will. There will be those in your life that regardless of what you do they will never believe you. As a matter of fact, there are those in your life that could watch you walk across Lake Erie, and they would go back and tell everyone that you can't swim. I know of people desperately trying to get everyone to believe in them, and often that leads to disaster.

On paper, Richard Nixon is probably one of the most accomplished presidents ever elected to the White House. He served in World War II, received his law degree, became Congressman and eventually Senator of California, and was the youngest vice president in United States history. However, many historians and biographers wrote that Nixon longed for the unanimous approval of others. Henry Kissinger once stated, *"Oh what a great man he would be if only he were loved"*. His desire to be accepted by all ultimately led Nixon to resign the White House in disgrace. The lesson to be learned from this story is, not everyone is going to believe in you, but if you believe in yourself and do the right things the right people will believe in you.

THE 4P'S OF YOU

It is important that you believe in yourself and have passion in your mission and purpose to the point that you recognize those that are your nonbelievers, and do not waste too much time trying to get them to believe. Actions always speak louder than words, and your actions will prove to the right people that you are capable of successfully completing your purpose.

When I was promoted to the leadership position at the community college that I worked for, there was one established member of the leadership team that did not want me on the team. As a matter of fact this colleague would constantly be dismissive in leadership meetings towards me. I never took it personally, but on the same note, I did want to show the ones that wanted me on the leadership team that they had made the right decision selecting me to be a part of it.

In one of our leadership meetings, I proposed a program in which, if successful, the department that I was in charge of would generate a substantial amount of additional revenue for the campus. For presenting this proposal in front of the entire leadership Council, I presented this plan to the leader of the Council in a private meeting. The leader of the Council approved of the plan and wanted me to propose it to the entire Council. The colleague who did not want me on the Council was trying desperately to make my proposal sound foolish. At one point this colleague asked a question about the proposal to the leader of the Council while I was still presenting as if I wasn't even there. The leader of the Council responded to my colleague by saying *"I don't know, ask him"*. This colleague refused to ask me the question directly.

My proposal was ultimately implemented by my department, and it was very successful. If you think that the success of my proposal proved to this dissenting colleague that I belonged on this counsel, you would be sadly mistaken. My colleague never acknowledged the success of the program and spent the rest of our time working together constantly trying to belittle me and my department. I learned to live with that. As long as I was doing my job effectively, my colleagues' attacks never affected my belief that my role on the Council was my obligation to my department.

Be encouraged by their discouragement

I may have learned how to deal with my fellow Council colleagues by experience that I had in high school. I graduated from Williamsville East High School in East Amherst, New York. However, because my parents were separated, I did attend Northview High School in Brazil, Indiana briefly. While attending that school, there was a teacher who I know did not like me. As far as I know, I did not give her any reason to dislike me, and to this day I cannot pinpoint one solid reason for the way she treated me. However, for some reason, the way she would treat me motivated me to excel in her class. My success in her class did not make this teacher happy. As a matter of fact, my success in her class would actually cause this woman to become passive-aggressive and literally tell other classmates during class time that they should not allow me to get the highest grades in class.

Because it seemingly made her angry, I would make sure I got the best grades in her class. One thing I was glad about is that most of the tests that she gave were true, false and multiple-choice so she could not be biased in grading my assignments. Though she did not like me, as an educator, I do respect the fact that she was honest in her grading procedures. I made an "A" in her class. For that semester, I was the only student that did so. How did I know that? She made it a point to ask the entire class *"How could you let Trunnis be the best student in this class?"* Though I will admit that that comment was one of the worst comments ever received from a teacher, I must also say that I left her classroom with a sense of satisfaction knowing that my success made her angry.

After that semester was over, I decided that I did not necessarily belong at Northview High School, and I longed to be back with my friends back in Western New York. That summer I had come back to visit my family in Brazil Indiana and ran into a student who attended the class with that teacher with me. Apparently, she had told the class that I'd quit school and that is why I was no longer in the course. Much to the surprise of that student, that was not the case at all.

I go to, Brazil, Indiana every year because I made a promise to my grandmother years ago that I would put flowers on the graves of all the family members buried in the cemeteries in Brazil after my grandmother passed away. In one of those Brazil, Indiana visits, I had to stop and get gas before I left town, and I happened to run into that teacher. We acknowledged each other, I introduced her to my children who came with me, and she asked me what I was doing for a living. At the time I had just become the academic chair for the business college in which I was teaching, so I told her what I was doing. Instead of congratulating me, or even asking me how I liked it, her reply to me was: *"Don't you need a graduate degree to do that?"* My reply was that not only do you need a graduate degree for my position, but you need a terminal degree as well. Before she could reply with any type of passive-aggressive comment, I replied with some self-deprecating, yet arrogant comment of *"I know, I guess they give those things to anyone"*.

When I received my doctorate degree, I remember my mother shedding tears of joy. Seeing my mother's reaction gave me a sense of accomplishment. However, the look of disbelief and near disgust on this teacher's face when she found out that I had a doctorate degree gave me a sense of satisfaction that almost motivated me to go back and get a second doctorate just so I could invite her to the graduation. For years, I thought this teacher may have treated me the way she did due to the color of my skin. However, years later I came to find out that she treated my sister-in-law who is white the exact same way, and in some cases even worse. So, though she still may have been racist, it's quite easy to determine that she was just very mean-spirited. Either way, her behavior towards me taught me more than anything that you can increase your passion to succeed by feeding off the energy of those who discourage you.

Those that bring out your passion

This segment of the book could easily be called the tale of two teachers. I graduated from Williamsville East High School in East Amherst, New York. The time of my graduation, the rate in which students went on to college was extremely high for that high school. What was even more amazing about that statistic was that Williamsville East was a public school, and usually the rate for students going on to college from high school is not as high in public schools as it is in private schools. That statistic within itself is evidence that the curriculum and the teachers at that high school could be considered elite, to say the least. One of all the teachers at Williamsville East, Bernadette Ruoff, was my English communications teacher. I had her for one class, for one semester, and it was one comment that she wrote on one of my assignments that helped change my approach to life forever.

It was my junior year of high school, and I had an assignment due in Mrs. Ruoff's class. I forgot what the assignment was, but I'm quite confident that I probably invested all of 30 minutes into this assignment. I turned the assignment in and received 80-something percent which would have equated to a "B". Not bad for not trying, right? However, Mrs. Ruoff wrote in red ink at the top of the assignment that she knew I had more potential than what I was displaying in her class. She went on to say that if I had given my hundred percent in her course that there was no doubt in her mind that I would be making an "A" in her class. As a 17-year-old, at first glance, all I saw was the passing grade and I went on with life.

However, one day I was doing homework at the kitchen table, and I had my folder open and that paper was visible for my father to see. My father read the comment and grounded me from my car for two weeks. He said that Mrs. Ruoff or any other teacher should not be pushing you to do your best. He went on to say that it should be what you do all the time, and not only does Mrs. Ruoff expect more effort, but he does also. At that point, Mrs. Ruoff became the meanest teacher on the planet in my opinion. However mean as she may be, I never received less than 90% on any of her assignments for the rest of the class.

Though as a shortsighted 17-year-old, I was very upset with Mrs. Ruoff, but as a man in my 50s, I'm really glad she wrote that comment. Her recognition of my potential eventually provided motivation and inspiration to serve my purpose and fuel my passion. Her comment calling me to display my full potential helped me at Navy boot camp when I was ready to give up. It helped me several times in my professional life when I was feeling a little lazy, and I knew I was not giving it my all. It also helped me in my personal life when there were moments when I just did not feel like moving forward. Whenever those moments came to me, or still come to me, I always remember her comments written in red ink demanding me to give it my all.

In my academic journey from kindergarten to PhD, I have had several instructors. One of the most valuable experiences I had during that journey of 16 weeks I was privileged to share with Mrs. Ruoff. I strongly believe that all successful and driven people should have a Mrs. Ruoff in their life to remind them of their full potential and push them to give it their all.

Sometimes on our journey to fulfill our purpose, we tend to get comfortable in our successes. For example, I know people who are on a diet and have a plan to lose 20 pounds, and when they lose that 20 pounds they go back to their comfort and gain 30 pounds. In those people's cases, it is important that there is someone to remind them how they felt when they were 20 pounds overweight. My brother David Goggins has made a living out of making sure to remind his followers the misery they experienced when they were in their comfort zone. Though sometimes done harshly, the overall transformation of many of his followers proves that harsh honesty fuels passion and leads to goal and purpose accomplishment.

Building your team

Previous stories I shared about people who fuel my passion were stories of people who entered my life by circumstance and random occurrences. However, this book is about intentionally discovering one's purpose and building a plan, so we will not focus on the random chance of meeting the right people. We will focus on building a network and will assist you in achieving your purpose with adequate assistance.

Skip Downing wrote a textbook for first-year college students called On Course. It is a great textbook that deals with issues of how to approach both life and college. One of the chapters addresses different types of people. Downing first talks about dependent people who rely on others for them to do most of the work in order for their goals to be achieved. He talks about codependent people which are those who will achieve the goals of others before they achieve their own. He labels independent people as those who will sacrifice some other goals in order for them to achieve a decent portion of their goals on their own. Finally, he talks about individuals who are interdependent. Those are individuals who believe in a balanced approach to achieving goals. They are very effective at giving and receiving help. Downing stated that achieving is a major step in achieving your goals.

I will take Downing's findings and go one step further. Building a network of interdependent people will not only assist you in achieving your goals, but an interdependent network can enhance your purpose and fuel your passion. When you are surrounded by a network of interdependent individuals, and you are interdependent as well, find joy in each other's success. You will also contribute to each other's success.

I always watch Buffalo Sabres hockey, but in this one game the player, Jeff Skinner, was one point away from reaching a milestone in career point totals. His entire team knew that, and throughout the entire game all tried diligently to ensure that Skinner achieved his point total milestone. Skinner achieved that milestone early on, and it seemed like the entire team rejoiced in his success genuinely. The Buffalo Sabres have suffered mightily in the NHL standings over the past several years. However, the new group of teammates seem to be very interdependent and are supportive of each other. This teamwork has led to recognizable success on the ice. For many years the Sabres have had some outstanding individuals on their team, but these individuals were more about themselves and less about the team. Fans of the Buffalo Sabres suffered mightily when the team roster was loaded with independent players only.

Building your network

Earlier in this book, I stressed the importance of needing people. Once again, I can't stress the importance of needing people enough. Say what you will about liking the song or not, Barbra Streisand was right when she said "people who need people are the luckiest people". Barbra Streisand should have gone on to say that you need the right people. Just to have people in your life may not be the best situation to put yourself in. Remember, you are living intentionally, and intentionally recruiting individuals in your personal and professional life is important for you to achieve your goals and purpose.

Once you understand and are committed to your purpose, and you have started formulating and executing your plan on achieving that purpose, you should look around at your personal associations. You want to make sure that the people around you in your personal life are there to enhance and complement your purpose. You do not want to have too many people who are dependent or codependent in their relationship with you.

A few years back, when I was program chair for the community college where I worked, I nominated a graduating student as business student of the year. That student won the award and was invited to the faculty/student dinner in which she was to receive that award. She brought her immediate family with her, and she presented them to me for an introduction. I remember shaking hands with her mother, and in greeting me she said *"So you are the one that is taking away my daughter"*. I was kind of taken aback, but then I realized her circumstances.

The student was the first in her family to attend college. This student's father had passed away when she and her sister were young, and the student, her sister, and her mother lived in a small town in a house that was next door to both her uncle and her grandmother. Her success and subsequent graduation would ultimately lead to this successful student finding a very good job and leaving the small town because of better opportunities and more metropolitan areas. This student's family did not depend on her for financial reasons, but they were dependent on her for emotional reasons. If this student would have succumbed to the emotions of her family, their dependency would've held her back from many opportunities. Instead, the student found a great balance between family and professional success and has gone on to become very successful in her field of work.

Though dependent and codependent people can impede your ultimate goal accomplishment, independent people in your network can be just as dangerous. Being independent is not necessarily a bad thing. In my experience, there are primarily two types of independent people: one type that have been raised that way and believe that independence is the only way to live life. The other type is the individual who may have been interdependent in the past but were hurt by others who took advantage of that person's giving side of their nature. As a result, this type of independent person may put up walls that are intentional in the prevention of not getting hurt in the same manner again. Either way, a solely independent person who is in an important position of your network can prove harmful in certain circumstances.

I have a lifelong friend, and years ago he was in a relationship with a rather charming woman. They both were in college and this woman was very open about wanting to do extensive traveling, on her own, around the world when she graduated college. She said she wanted to take an extensive amount of time off before finally settling down with a career and a *"normal life"*. She was an extremely kind person with an independent spirit.

It was clear that my friend thought that she was the one for him, and he started making decisions and plans that would benefit both. However, that is not what his girlfriend wanted. His girlfriend was very open about her independence. Shortly before he graduated college, his girlfriend decided that the relationship was going in a direction that was not to her benefit, and she broke it off. My friend was devastated since he made significant alterations to his life plan in order to make sure that his girlfriend was included. He constantly blamed her for misleading him. However, that was not the case at all. She was extremely open about her plans, and according to mutual friends, she felt no remorse about breaking off their relationship.

I'm sharing the story because when building your personal network, it is imperative that you ensure that every relationship is mutually beneficial. Always ensure that all relationships are interdependent in nature and both you and the other party are actively listening to each other to make sure that the needs and purpose of all individuals are being met. If there is not a significant amount of active listening, relationships within your potential network can possibly end up like my dear friend's.

Get involved

Another way you can feel your passion is to get involved and stay involved in your community. Go out, volunteer and be active in your community. When I teach inmates who served time for drug offenses, I often encourage them to either volunteer or become a paid recovery coach. These individuals who are getting out of prison are extremely motivated to stay clean, but with addiction, there is always that temptation. One way to help steer these individuals away from a relapse is to help others in their addiction. I know of several former inmates in which being a recovery coach has helped in their own long-term recovery.

Professionally, it is also important that you join societies that are associated with the industry that you are working in and do research and other activities that directly contribute to the betterment of your industry or discipline. This is a great way to stay involved and increase the passion that you have in achieving your purpose. This type of involvement will also allow you the opportunity to find ways to improve yourself and your strategic plan.

Chapter 13

Persistence

You have read 12 chapters of this book so far, and you have already developed your plan, established your purpose, and you have built a network of individuals that will help you in achieving all your goals. It is now smooth sailing from here. Right? No, executing your plan and achieving your purpose, now that it is determined, will be the hardest and longest journey you will have. Your passion that you have for achieving your purpose can now add to your stress levels. Because you've invested so much time, the stakes to your success have now become high. There will be challenges, and with those challenges it is imperative that you have the will to keep moving forward.

Though I am saying what you already know, I must stress that there will be pitfalls and challenges in the achievement of your goals and your purpose. There are internal pitfalls such as self-doubt, and procrastination. Self-doubt can almost stall someone from moving forward on their goals. Procrastination on the other hand can prevent you from even starting your journey at all. When I talk to students and to business leaders that I consult, the two biggest obstacles to goal and purpose achievement are self-doubt and procrastination.

THE 4P'S OF YOU

When I was working on my PhD dissertation, I knew that the absence of an organized class structure would cause me to procrastinate in completing my dissertation and meeting my projected timeline to finish my degree. Because I recognize this weakness, I reached out to a cousin of mine who was already successful academically. His attitude and mine didn't really mesh well, and I knew that if I got him involved in my dissertation process he would say snarky things to me that would motivate me to finish my dissertation and complete it in a timeline faster than he finished his. That did seem to work, and I was able to overcome my procrastination and finish my dissertation in a timely manner.

Overcoming self-doubt, on the other hand, is somewhat harder. I've dealt with many college students who when overcome with self-doubt those students tend to fall away from the dream of obtaining a college degree. This also happens in other areas of our life as well. We all regret passing up an opportunity in our past due to the fact that we underestimated our ability to achieve that opportunity. I know many times I've talked myself out of both personal and professional opportunities because I doubted my ability to be successful.

There are also several external pitfalls as well. These pitfalls are outside of your control and often time it could be simply you being at the wrong place at the wrong time. Back in 1989, the Pennsylvania lottery hit a record $115 million jackpot. I was living in Buffalo at the time, and my father and I decided to drive an hour from Buffalo to the Pennsylvania State line after I'd gotten out of school. As my father and I were driving down to the state line, I was looking at license plates trying to select numbers to put on the lottery tickets. When we got halfway to Stateline, we got a flat tire. We had to pull over and change the tire which delayed our time getting to the store to buy the tickets. By the time we got to the store, the line was extremely long. We stood in line, but unfortunately, the machines shut down at 7 o'clock. We were unable to purchase the lottery tickets.

On our way home from Pennsylvania, we decided to stop at a truck stop to get a bite to eat. Now back then, Pennsylvania used to draw their lottery numbers almost immediately after their lottery machines shut down. So while sitting in the truck stop, my dad and I got to see the numbers from the drawing. At the piece of paper in which I wrote down all the lottery numbers, and to my astonishment, I had selected every single number. There were multiple winners of that lottery that night, and if I were to have gotten a ticket, I would've had a portion of $115 million. Though I was extremely disappointed at the time, this served as a lesson in the future that sometimes you can do everything you're supposed to do to reach her goal. However, sometimes there are forces that are outside of your control that can interfere with your success and progress. I will share a little bit more about overcoming pitfalls like this in the next chapter. However, it is important to know that external pitfalls will happen.

THE 4P'S OF YOU

Must move forward

I will say that when my father and I did not win the lottery that spring day in Pennsylvania, I was very disappointed. However, I got up and went to school the next day and moved on with my life. In order to be successful in life, you must be able to move forward. When I coached Little League hockey, I remember when kids would have a really good shot on goal, and would think that they were going to score, but the opposing goalie miraculously saved the shot from crossing the goal line and going into the net. Some of the kids I coached would look up into the rafters, and almost stop skating in disbelief. Once I saw that, I would immediately call for them to get off the ice. The reason for that is they have stopped moving forward, and that disappointment may cloud their judgment for the rest of the shift. Once they got back to the bench, I would go over to them and tell them to shake it off and think about the next shift and the success that they could have then.

Sometimes that's what we must do when we are faced with disappointment. There are times when we have to get off the *"ice"* because disappointment has slowed us down and caused us to momentarily *"stop skating"*. In my brother's book **You can't hurt me,** there are a number of stories that he shares of moving forward. He overcame the familial and racial trials of his childhood, his physical trials after his service in the Air Force to go on and become a very successful Navy Seal.

This book has inspired countless people. Basically, it shows that through all of the trials and tribulations that David went through, the powers that be were never able to hurt him and he went on to become a very successful individual. With that being said, for those who read the book and believe that they can no longer be hurt, I will say that it is okay to hurt. However, it is important that you are able to play hurt. My brother is and has always been a unique individual. His tolerance and standards are very unique as well. It is important that you are able to recognize your tolerance and accept the fact that pain is a part of humanity. I've learned over the years that it is okay to hurt, as long as you keep moving forward.

If you've read just the first chapter of this book, you would know that I'm a huge Buffalo Bills fan. Though the Buffalo Bills have had Hall of Fame quarterbacks like Jack Kemp and Jim Kelly, and a future Hall of Famer and Josh Allen, no quarterback in Buffalo Bills history has had as much of an impact on my life as Joe Ferguson. Ferguson was quarterback of the Buffalo Bills through almost my entire childhood. He experienced some mighty lean years playing with that team. However in the early 80s, the Buffalo Bills experienced some regular-season success. The 1980 season was a first in my lifetime when I watched the Buffalo Bills beat the Miami Dolphins. They finished that season 11-5, they won the AFC East, and went on to the playoffs to play San Diego Chargers.

THE 4P'S OF YOU

That playoff game against the San Diego Chargers had a profound impact on the rest of my life. It was not because of the game itself, but it was because of the actions of Joe Ferguson. Joe Ferguson played that game on a sprained ankle. Ferguson was barely able to walk back to the huddle in between plays. However, once the ball was snapped, he ran and moved as if nothing was wrong with his ankle. He played through intense pain. Did the Bills go on to win? No, it is still the Buffalo Bills. They are clearly the Chicago Cubs of the NFL. However, Joe Ferguson's display of courage left a lifelong impression that regardless of the pain you are going through, you must press forward and finish the game. That can be something as simple as a football, hockey, or basketball game; or it can be something as important as the game of life.

On June 19, 2015, the game that was played on January 3, 1981, once again came into the forefront of my mind. At 11 o'clock that night, I received a call that my oldest daughter had been shot. I had just fallen asleep when I received the call, and by far there has never been a set of words that has shocked me or stunned me in such a way. I immediately got up and went to the scene thinking that my daughter was transported to a hospital, but she was not. I remember the initial officer telling me that no one had been sent to hospital. My legal experience working with the Indiana Atty. Gen., and my military experience led me to surmise that my daughter did not survive her wounds.

I remember waiting for hours for the coroner to come so I could identify her. I remember everything about that night. I remember the sounds, the smell, the tears, and the utter confusion. I also remember for the first time ever feeling totally helpless and lost. I felt a pain that I could not describe. It was a mental anguish that literally led to nausea. I also remember that with all of the thoughts that went through my head that night, the vision of Joe Ferguson limping back to the huddle, then limping to the line, but then running the plays he called in spite of his pain stood out. As a matter fact, it was that vision that allowed me to get through the loss of my daughter.

For those reading this who have lost a child, understand that the pain of losing a child is indescribable. It truly never goes away. For some that have lost children, they succumb to the pain and eventually the pain costs them their lives as well. Many times, after the loss of a child, the family unit is further impacted by substance abuse, mental illness, and divorce. Some of these instances did occur after Kayla's death. However, regardless of the pain, my family for the most part kept moving. Like Joe Ferguson, many of us limp to the huddle and limp back to the line of scrimmage, but when we say the proverbial *"hike"* that starts our day, we run the play effectively and we stay in the game. Though we all know that just as the Chargers won that game, we know life will eventually win over us as well. However, like Joe Ferguson, the ability to carry on and leave a positive impact for others for many years to come is the actual victory that can be achieved.

THE 4P'S OF YOU

Many people today are afraid of pain and failure. And though it is often unpleasant, pain does lead to growth and maturity. If you are a history buff, you know the story of Richard Nixon and his presidency. He is the only president in our nation's history, (so far), to resign from office. When discussing pitfalls, one can surmise that Nixon's pitfall was indeed internal in nature. It comes to disappointment and failure, Richard Nixon said one of the most thoughtful statements when it comes to how to handle pain and disappointment. This is a statement that I often share with students and others when they are going through a challenging time. Nixon said, *"because the greatness comes not when things go always good for you, but the greatness comes when you are really tested, when you take some knocks, some disappointments, when sadness comes; because only if you've been in the deepest valley can you ever know how magnificent it is to be on the highest mountain."* Though Richard Nixon is not known for his honesty in the White House, no truer words have ever been spoken by an American President.

Seemingly as a former president, Nixon found some redemption. He was an informal consultant to Presidents Ford through Clinton. He wrote a number of books on foreign policy and politics. Through perseverance and determination, Richard Nixon was, (at least on the surface), able to overcome the pain in disgrace of Watergate. There are other times that you will not be able to get over pain. There are other times you will just have to deal with it.

My father was an extremely smart and practical man, but he was far from sentimental. I remember calling my father when my first wife and I were going through our separation and subsequent divorce. I remember sharing with him the pain I was going through because I really wanted a family that stayed together, and I felt robbed of that opportunity. I remember the fragile emotional state that I was in at the time. When I finished pouring my heart out, my father so eloquently responded *"deal with it"*. At the time, I thought that had to be the coldest response I ever could have received under the circumstances. However, as I grow older and experienced more setbacks and disappointments as we all do, I grew to realize that in some circumstances all you can to is "deal with it" because sometimes that circumstance, (divorce, death, serious health issues, etc.) will not get better and you must learn to operate, (*"deal"* if you will), with that disappointing circumstance being part of your new reality.

Deal with it, is what Joe Ferguson did when he willed himself to finish that playoff game. Deal with it is what I have to do when dealing with the painful anguish regarding the death of my daughter. And deal with it is what you must do when faced with circumstances that you cannot change. Remember these are obstacles that you must overcome in order to achieve your purpose. I was well into adulthood before I knew the true meaning of *"deal with it"*. However, some learn to deal with it far earlier in life, and are better for it.

THE 4P'S OF YOU

On April 6, 2018, a team bus carrying the Humboldt Broncos, a Junior ice hockey team from Saskatchewan, was hit by a tractor-trailer. The accident killed 16 people and seriously injured 13 others that were on the team bus. It was indeed a tragic moment not only for the sport of hockey but for the entire nation of Canada. Many on that bus had dreams of furthering their career in the great sport of hockey and for those players injured, you can't help but wonder if they think about what could have been. One player particularly decided not to wonder what it could've been. He decided very early on about what he was going to be.

Ryan Straschnitzki was one of the hockey players seriously injured in that bus crash. He suffered a spinal injury that left him paralyzed. Ryan had dreams from an early age to become a successful hockey player, and up until the bus crash, he was well on his way to finding success. However, immediately after that bus crash, Ryan had to deal with the fact that he may never be able to play hockey at a professional level let alone walk again. At his young age, I'm sure that this reality was devastating. Ryan had a choice at that moment to either give up on his purpose, or *"deal with it"* and achieve his purpose in any way he could.

Today Ryan is still playing hockey and still fighting for the right to represent Canada on an international stage. He wears his Canada jersey with pride and is hopeful that he will be on the 2026 Paralympic sled hockey team. Without question, the setback Ryan received was devastating. It is reasonable to believe that this young man experienced tremendous disappointment if not full out depression. However, Ryan found the strength and the persistence to *"deal with it"*, and five years after his tragic event he is still striving to serve his purpose. Though I am a proud participant and contributor to USA hockey, I will admit that in 2026 I will be cheering Ryan on to deliver the gold-medal to his nation.

Persistence and disappointment

We live in a society now where disappointment is treated in ways that do not allow people to benefit from the experience of disappointment. Though I do believe that drugs to treat mental health are necessary, I do not necessarily agree with some doctors proposing this as the first option in treating depression. Immediately after my daughter passed away, it is understandable that I was in a state of despair. I felt lost and depressed and empty, and I explained my condition to my doctor. He immediately recommended that I take an antidepressant. I looked at the doctor and asked, *"Will these pills bring my daughter back"*. He looked at me as if I were crazy and said nervously *"no"*. Then I responded to him *"then why take it because when the effects of the pill wear off the problem will still remain"*. To treat my disappointment by doing whatever I could to help others deal with their pain of loss. I also decided through healthy exercise and socialization to stay focused on the good things of life.

I know I shared Richard Nixon's farewell speech earlier in this chapter. I highly encourage you to watch that speech it is readily available online. Another line that is great to remember from that speech, especially dealing with disappointment is: *We think that when someone dear to us dies, we think that when we lose an election, we think that when we suffer defeat, that all is ended. We think, as T.R. said, that the light had left his life forever. Not true. It is only a beginning always.*

As unfortunate as this reality is today, many adults are still traumatized by their first disappointment which may have been their parents separation and divorce. I will admit that for many years in my life, I wondered what life would have been if my parents would have stayed together. However, like Richard Nixon said, it was not the end, it was a beginning. For my mother, it was the beginning of her journey of becoming an outstanding educator. For my brother it was the beginning of living his lifelong dream of becoming a Navy Seal. For my father, a reconciliation of the hardships he faced in life and the recognition of what truly is important. For me it was the beginning of a relationship with an outstanding person in Dana Garrett that though it was 30 years in the making, it was well worth finding a partner and warrior who patiently and steadfastly has stood by me. If my mother, father, brother, and myself viewed the separation of our family as an ending none of us would've achieved our purposes. I am not saying to look at your spouse right now and break up, but what I am saying is to not to look at disappointment as an ending, but as possibly a new direction in the path to achieving your purpose.

Persistence is about moving forward with your goals despite obstacles. On your path to achieving your purpose, you will suffer disappointments, you will have to change direction, and you will possibly have to take devastating hits. But as Rocky Balboa said, *"How hard you can hits; it's about how hard I hit you can take and keep moving forward"*. That is how winning is done.

Chapter 14

The Contingency Plan

In 1985, a man by the name of David Cook opened what would become the largest video store the nation has ever seen, Blockbuster Video. Due to his innovative ideas and concepts, Cook was able to secure major investors and by 1987 Cook left Blockbuster video a very wealthy man. By the 1990s, Blockbuster video was a major part of the late 20th century American family. However, Blockbuster was seemingly unaware of the happenings surrounding them, and eventually Blockbuster was a victim of its own inflexibility.

Blockbuster took the external threats to its company lightly. By the late 1990s, companies like Netflix and Redbox offered favorable alternatives to Blockbuster. In addition, Blockbuster underestimated the consumer interest in Internet streaming. By the time Blockbuster made modifications to their business plan, it was too late to be a viable player in the movie and entertainment industry. As a result, Blockbuster, who once had over 6000 retail stores around the world now only has one in Bend, Oregon. As a matter of fact, a company that Blockbuster had a chance of buying, (Netflix), now has a comedy series mocking its one-time rival.

Contingency planning and modification

The last chapter was about persistence and moving forward with your plan, even playing through the pain. This chapter is about contingency planning. Sometimes things will happen in your life or in your career that will require you to be persistent, to stop, self-reflect, and make necessary modifications, and even redirections to your plan and your purpose. I shared the story about Blockbuster because as one can see, in the beginning, Blockbuster had a phenomenal plan. David Cook's plan and idea turned a mom-and-pop video store into an industry giant in a very brief period of time. However, the company did not recognize things around them were changing in the way of technology and consumer behavior. As a result of not recognizing the external evolution, Blockbuster failed.

Today the company is owned by Dish Network, and every so often we see in business and entertainment news that Blockbuster is planning some sort of comeback. That remains to be seen. However, the most important part of this Blockbuster story is to always be aware of your changing environment and have the internal humility and wherewithal to make modifications to your plan and purpose.

Don't plan in a bubble

It is not uncommon to plan just thinking about your own actions. It is important to think about counter-actions that will or could occur while going about your plan. Making a plan in life is very much like game planning for a football game. In football, depending upon the situation, teams must switch up their personnel. For example, if a team is playing a game against a team that has a poor run defense, the opposing team may implement a game plan that is heavy on running the football. As a matter fact, they may sit some receivers and dress more running backs to plan for that occurrence. If the modifications were not made, it is quite possible that the opposing team would either miss out on an opportunity to exploit the other team's weakness, or worse yet they may lose because though the opposing team is weak on stopping the run, they may have a superior pass defense.

Things can go wrong

We all know the story about the Titanic. At the time, the planners and builders of this vessel had built the most technologically advanced ship of its kind ever. They were so confident in its technological advances they deemed the ship to be unsinkable and as a demonstration of their confidence, the builders did not have the number of lifeboats necessary to save everyone that was aboard the ship.

The ship sank on its maiden voyage. It hit an iceberg that though it didn't breach the whole of the ship, it did cause enough damage to negatively affect the watertight integrity of a vast portion of the ship. As a result, the Titanic sank rather quickly. Like the planners and investors of Blockbuster, the builders of the

Titanic had an unreasonable level of confidence in their plan. Their internal confidence in themselves caused them to not lend the necessary consideration to external focuses around them. In the case of the Titanic, there was no real contingency plan, and as a result, many innocent individuals faced an untimely demise.

Things do go wrong, and it is imperative that you plan for it. I want you to think about it this way. In the United States, around 31 to 35% of marriages end in divorce. In Canada, 40 to 60% of marriages end in divorce. With that being said, in the United States 65 to 69% of those who made long-term plans and developed a joint purpose with their spouse did not have to make a contingency plan for if they were alone. And in Canada, 40 to 60% did not need a contingency plan. However, there were a vast number of North Americans who had to prepare for life after marriage. To sound even more fatalistic, out of the 50 to 69% of those who do not experience divorce, 100% of those couples will lose their spouse due to death. So even those who planned and set goals with their spouse would eventually have to face the fact that they will have to do some of this journey in life on their own.

Nothing lasts forever. You should never prepare for *"what if"*, you should always prepare for *"when"*. The Titanic claimed it was unsinkable, and never prepared for when it would sink. Blockbuster prepared for video store dominance and never prepared for advanced technologies. It is imperative that when planning you should always have measures in place for when major or minor changes interfere with your plan and purpose.

Making adjustments

In 2008, as I was finishing up on my Masters degree and preparing to leave the Navy, my plan was to move back to Buffalo and work in finance. However, by the summer of 2008 I quickly realized that the financial situation not only in New York but around the world was not conducive to me starting a career in finance. As a result of that conclusion, I decided to get into higher education. This adjustment of mine proved to be an extremely wise decision not only for 2008, for the present.

I came to this decision by going back and reviewing my personal SWOT analysis. I looked at my strengths, weaknesses, and threats. As far as opportunities back in 2008, colleges and universities at that time were receiving massive enrollments due to the fact that many people were going back to school to reeducate and find new careers primarily because the great recession caused major damage to many of the industries in which these new nontraditional students had lost employment.

Like I said several chapters ago, never be married to your plan. You must always look for changes and adjustments. You must always keep it fresh. My father owned a nightclub in Buffalo, New York called the Vermillion Room. This nightclub was an extremely popular nightclub not only in Buffalo but in Western New York and Southern Ontario. It was often frequented by Buffalo Bills players like JD Hill, Haven Moses, O.J. Simpson, and my favorite Reggie McKenzie, (I might want to add that Reggie McKenzie is my favorite football player of all time because at one time he was our next-door neighbor). It was also a spot where celebrities like Stevie Wonder, Chaka Khan, Ike and Tina Turner, and Sister Sledge would go when they were in town. My father's nightclub was also the primary hangout spot for the undisputed King of Funk Rick James. My father's club had a reputation of being one of the most popular adult hangout spots in town in the '70s and '80s. However, like all popular nightclubs, the Vermillion Room lost its luster, and instead of my father forcing tradition down the throats of Buffaloians, my father decided to shut down the nightclub, completely remodel and rename it Wall Street.

Wall Street never rose to the level of popularity of the Vermillion Room, it did however offer its customers a change of scenery. My father did enjoy a level of success with the new club. My father's nightclub days were extended by his adjustments. I think my father knew that without those adjustments the music at 27 E. Ferry Street would have been quieted long before he would've wanted it to.

It is important that you build alternatives into your initial plan. These alternatives can serve as safety valves for when major changes to your internal and external environment arise. Having these alternatives are not because you are planning for failure, those alternatives are there because you are planning for sustained success.

Have a Plan B and C

It is imperative that you stick with your plan, but never be tied to your plan. In my Blockbuster video example, I demonstrated how not having flexibility in your plan can lead to unfavorable results. I'm not saying to not remain true to your purpose, but I am saying that you must be willing to make necessary modifications in order to make sure your purpose remains relevant.

A great example in modifying your plans but being true to your purpose is the company Body by Fisher. Fisher started out as a company that manufactured horse-drawn carriages in the late 1800s. The Fisher brothers quickly realized that the automobile was indeed the way of the future, and modified their buggy designs so that they could become car chassis. In the 20th century, Fisher forged a deal with General Motors to design several of General Motors car chassis. This modification allowed Body by Fisher to remain a viable business until the early 21st century when they finally dissolved. If this modification had not been made, Fisher would have gone out of business when all the other buggy companies folded many years ago.

Part of being persistent is being prepared and mindful of the constant state of change. Though you should always have a strategic mindset, it is imperative that you have a reactive or tactical plan in place for situations that may be outside your control. I was in grad school while in the Navy, and though my plan was to move back to Buffalo and start a career in finance, I also realized the risk involved in that industry and the fact that I had a large family to raise. As a result, I intentionally took electives in undergrad that would make my transcript favorable to a career in education.

This backup plan that I developed came in handy because shortly before I graduated with my MBA, the recession of 2008 started. Since I had made preparations in case my original plan fell through, it wasn't entirely difficult to pivot toward a degree. In order to do that I had to repurpose one of my social networks.

One of the most important social networks that I had during my time in undergrad and grad school was the staff and faculty of Marian College and Anderson University. In addition, as a Navy recruiter, I developed networks with academic and career advisors at Ivy Tech Community College and various other colleges in central Indiana. This network became a strength in my decision to transition to higher education. One individual in particular, Victoria Buzash, took a chance and allowed me to start teaching as an adjunct in her department at Ivy Tech- Indianapolis. From there I was allowed to build the experience necessary to grow in the industry of higher education.

Though I have enjoyed a successful career in higher education, I still dabble in and am open to using my skills and experience in other areas like business and education consulting and other fields. I do this to stay diverse professionally, and because I am completely aware that like all industries, higher education has its ebbs and flows. Today's enrollment numbers are not even close to the enrollment numbers that existed when I started in higher education. I am aware that this and other factors may have an affect on my career path and I must be prepared.

This scenario leads me to my next point in persistence which is that you must have multiple streams of income. The days of working for the same company, (even the same industry), are long gone. Today, according to the United States Bureau of Labor Statistics, the average employee stays on a job a little over four years. With technology, our economy is in a constant state of change, and it is imperative for all of us to constantly be looking to either improve or expand our labor skills in order to remain competitive in the workforce. Today more than ever, it is imperative that you always have a plan B because at any given time your income stream from plan A can dry up.

If plan "A" fails

There is a popular saying that *"if plan "A" fails there are 25 other letters in the alphabet"*. Though that is a very positive and uplifting mantra, it may not necessarily be realistic. In some cases, if you must create 25 alternative plans, you may have not put too much time in your initial plan in the first place. In addition, your skill set may not allow you to have a wide variety of options. For example, if you are a skilled automotive engineer, your skill set may allow you to get into aviation or similar fields, but could that skill set make you a successful accountant? Not saying that it can't be done, but it is an option that may be way outside of one's wheelhouse.

Don't force a purpose

Back in 1982, singer Jennifer Holliday had a song called and I am telling you I'm not going. The song was extremely popular and was a top R&B hit and charted on the Billboard Hot 100 and UK singles chart. Her song even won a Grammy. I remember the song was extremely popular during couples-only skates at my father's skating rink. The song was an extremely popular ballad.

The song came out when I was 11, at the time I didn't really understand the lyrics. Also, the song drifted into the obscurity of my brain, and I forgot about it. Years later I was driving down the interstate on a road trip and I heard the song. Due to the fact that I haven't heard in a long time, I decided to stop channel surfing and listen. As an adult, I heard and understood the lyrics, and came up with a very different feeling regarding this song.

First, I want to say that Holliday has a beautiful voice, and is delightful to the ears. However, the lyrics to this song really had me thinking. Song starts out by her saying *"you're the best man I'll ever know/there's no way I can ever go"* she's adamant about staying in the relationship, and at one point she asked her man *"please stay and hold me, Mr. Mann try it mister, try it Mr. I know, I know, I know you can"*. The song states that there's no way that she's living without her man, and the last line of the song is "you're gonna love me". Clearly this song is about a woman who loves a man dearly. Frankly, the lyrics are obsessed. If a woman sang that song to me, it is quite possible that I would obtain a restraining order, and notify her of that restraining order only after I had gotten a considerable distance away from her and started a new life.

A few chapters back I talked about passion if not balanced could lead to obsession. The same can be with persistence. It is great to be persistent in obtaining and achieving your purpose. Be mindful of the danger of trying to force a purpose that was never meant to be. I don't know the total back story of the Jennifer Holliday song, but the lyrics are indicative of an individual who is trying to convince a lover that a relationship can work regardless of the sacrifice and cost. The song even indicates that regardless of what the man says or does, she will always be there. Though this comes from a position of love, it opens the door for the singer to be taken advantage of and even harmed.

Though not all of us do this in love relationships, we can all go back to a time where we tried to force a purpose. Recently my son Zachary did not make the final cut of a hockey team that he desired to be rostered. Zachary thought that because he was on the team the year before, he was almost assured a roster spot. However, for whatever reason, Zachary lost that spot to another goalie, and was regulated to the Indiana State player pool for hockey. He was quickly picked up by another high school in need of a goaltender.

Without question, Zachary was extremely disappointed to not play for the team that he played for the year before. Though he had to experience this on his own, I can see from the interaction that he had with his coaches and I had with the team manager that he was not going to be a member of the hockey team that he desired to play on for long. Throughout the entire summer, Zachary would practice with his former teammates in order to be prepared for tryouts. When he found out that he did not make the team, he was surprised and heartbroken.

Zachary has been a goaltender virtually his entire hockey career, and being cut by his desired team caused him to seriously consider changing positions in order to make the team. Zachary had done well as a goaltender and was even getting recognized by private colleges in the Midwest. If Zachary chained positions at such a late stage, it would have jeopardized his chances at playing college hockey. However, in the beginning, Zachary felt that it was his purpose to play for the hockey team he truly desired.

After consultation, Zachary did decide to play for the hockey team that selected him in the pool. He had a spectacular season and even won Indiana's Commissioners Cup shutting out the rival high school. Though disappointing, Zachary accepted a change in purpose, and by accepting this change, his performance enhanced his college portfolio for hockey that much more.

Though it is important to be persistent, it is okay to accept that some things are not meant to be. It is equally important to recognize when it is time to accept that fate. Every goal in every purpose will have challenges and tribulation. However, forced outcomes and challenges are different. Overcoming challenges when achieving your purpose leads to long-term satisfaction. However, forcing outcomes leads to long-term anxiety of future loss.

Okay to start over

It is absolutely okay to start over when things do not go quite as planned. I have given a ton of sports analogies, and we are too late in the book for me to stop now. However this analogy has nothing to do with Buffalo sports. Tim Tebow was an outstanding college quarterback. In 2009, Tebow led the Florida Gators to a national championship. He was drafted a year later by the Denver Broncos. Though he led the Broncos to the NFL playoffs in 2011, even beating the Pittsburgh Steelers in a thrilling playoff game, the Broncos did not believe that Tim Tebow was their future franchise quarterback. After the 2011 season, the Broncos signed Peyton Manning and parted ways with Tebow. He signed on with the New York Jets, but he was unable to convince the Jets that he was their quarterback either. He went on to be on the Patriots and Eagles roster, but again his quarterback career never took off.

Despite the disappointment of not fully living the dream of becoming a franchise quarterback, Tebow has enjoyed success as a broadcaster and a professional baseball player for the New York Mets organization. He even has enjoyed some success as a filmmaker by being the executive producer of a sports movie in 2019 called **Run the Race**. In 2021, Tebow did try to come back in the NFL as a tight end for the Jacksonville Jaguars. Though he did have a respectable preseason, he did not make the final roster. Tim Tebow knew his purpose was to be an athlete and an important contributor in sports, and though he was not a Super Bowl winning quarterback, he has contributed to sports in general in many ways.

Tebow's example is a prime example of how it is important to utilize your skills in a way where they can be important in contingency planning. It is important to not force your purpose. Forcing your purpose will ultimately lead to misery. It is always important to recognize the fine line between persistence and obsession.

Chapter 15

There Will Be Pain Regardless

Pain is inevitable. Whether it be physical, emotional, or professional, discomfort and hardship are parts of the human experience. However, the presence of pain does not have to mark the end of effort or ambition. Instead, it should serve as a reminder that meaningful pursuits often come with some level of struggle. In this chapter, I want to share both personal and professional insights that have shaped my perspective on this truth.

Nancy Little is a prime example of perseverance in the face of physical adversity. I met Nancy while playing co-ed beer league hockey in Indianapolis. Anyone who's played in this environment knows it can be intense, physical, and surprisingly competitive. Although there aren't as many women as men in these leagues, the women who do play stand out—not only because of their toughness but because of the camaraderie they foster. Nancy quickly became a staple on the ice and within our circle.

She wasn't just a participant—she was a force. Nancy was aggressive, tenacious, and, as we joked, occasionally 'dirty' in the most playful and strategic sense. She didn't hesitate to hack your shins if you were in her way. Off the ice, she was the life of the tournament, often in charge of refreshments, and always the person who made sure everyone felt like part of the team. She was over 60 when I first met her, but you wouldn't know it from her energy and physicality.

During a warm-up conversation before a game, I learned Nancy was a grandmother. I was shocked—not just because of her youthful appearance, but because of her sheer drive and resilience. We talked about aging and the toll hockey takes on our bodies. Both of us acknowledged the pain we carried—nagging injuries, sore joints, and aging muscles—but agreed there was nothing quite like being on the ice with teammates, reliving our youth and pushing past the discomfort. That was nearly eight years ago. Nancy is now closing in on 70—and still plays.

Her story demonstrates an important truth: if you avoid one kind of pain, you often open the door to another. I've seen countless friends stop exercising due to one injury, only to develop more serious health conditions like obesity, diabetes, or cardiovascular issues. Avoiding short-term discomfort can lead to long-term suffering. The same is true emotionally and professionally.

Emotionally, many people shut down after heartbreak. I've seen people swear off love following divorce or rejection. They tell themselves they'll never go through that kind of pain again, but what they often find instead is loneliness, depression, and isolation. In an effort to avoid one wound, they suffer another that's deeper and more lasting. Life was never meant to be lived in solitude—not when we are wired for connection, for risk, for hope.

Instead of swearing off love, this is a great time to go back and think about what happened in that relationship, what happened in that rejection that could have been done differently. I'm not saying jump right back into a relationship, but I am saying learned from that relationship and make sure you do it better next time. Make sure you're not doing the same thing that you were doing last time that causes that pain. My grandmother used to say that you never find your spouse in a bar. As I got older, I found out that they may not be at a bar, sometimes not even at church, but they're definitely not your workplace. I say that jokingly, but that may be where the heartache began is where you found your significant other. Another thing is to look for warning signs. Remember I talked about how I went through three divorces, but I came to realize that I was the one causing the pain through forcing purpose, there may be certain things that you are doing that are creating painful circumstances that can be avoided. Once you overcome those circumstances, you can overcome pain.

Professionally, I've encountered individuals who gave up after a single rejection—a missed promotion, a failed interview, or a lost opportunity. Rather than persist, they remained stuck, their growth stunted by the bitterness of one moment. They built their own glass ceilings, sealing themselves off from possibilities they might have achieved had they pushed through that initial pain.

In some cases, people do not achieve promotion because they are really too good at what they're doing for organization at the position they currently hold. This is very selfish for the organization to prevent someone from moving forward, but it happens often. Maybe sometimes your promotion is to leave the organization and go somewhere else. I know that that may be a form of starting over. And you may feel very comfortable in your place of employment. However, by giving this circumstance in the situation and the hypothetical that I just presented, maybe that organization doesn't care enough about you to allow you to grow to your full potential. Sometimes it is a hard decision but is a decision that needs to be made. Now again the pain of discomfort and leaving an organization is an additional pain, but it will not be the pain of regret and bitterness knowing that you were capable of doing so much more and decided not to.

The truth is pain is not optional. It's part of the journey. What *"is"* optional is how we respond to it. We can either let it paralyze us or propel us. Personally, I live with chronic physical pain from past sports injuries. I also carry emotional pain, like everyone else. But I've learned that staying still only invites more discomfort—more regret, more lost time, more missed chances.

You may be reading this during your own painful season—whether in your body, your heart, or your career. If so, I want to encourage you: keep moving. Get up. Apply again. Love again. Try again. You're going to experience pain either way—so why not choose the pain that leads to something greater? Risk brings reward. Effort brings growth.

Nancy's story still motivates me. She plays through her pain because she knows what's on the other side: joy, connection, and vitality. I hope her story—and mine—give you the push you need. Let your pain shape you, not stop you. Let it remind you that you're alive and that there is still more ahead. Choose your pain—don't let it choose you.

Chapter 16

Time to Relax

Spring of 2014, I had a full plate of issues. Professionally I was working on getting a college degree that was nationally accredited to achieve regional accreditation. My father had just died in November of the previous year, and I was trying to handle the issues revolving around the aftermath of his passing. Academically, I was still working on finishing my dissertation and was in the research stage which required me to travel throughout the state of Indiana. To top it all off, in January 2014 I became aware that my daughter, (not yet graduated high school), was pregnant. It was imperative at that time to help navigate her through a difficult time in her life. I worked very hard to try not to drop the ball on all of the issues going on at that time. However, I was losing lots of sleep, and though I did not tell anyone I was extremely overwhelmed.

In the midst of my storm, I set a counseling appointment with Pastor Philip Meade of Caring Place church in Indianapolis, Indiana. During our very first counseling session, my cell phone must've rung eight times. All these calls were calls regarding things that I had to deal with like things at work, things at home, and even things dealing with my dissertation. Pastor Meade was very quiet during this time, and when I finished talking, he looked at me and said you *"need to find somewhere to go; a place no one knows where you are, you need to think, you need to sit, and if necessary, you need to let out a loud scream"*. He went on to say that I was taking care of everyone's needs but my own. He was emphatic that I needed time to myself.

I never found the place that Pastor Meade described. Quite frankly, I have too much energy just to go somewhere and sit down. However eventually, I found an activity that was an adequate substitute, and that was bike riding. Exercise releases endorphins that really help in calming an individual down. The Sunday after my daughter passed away, and everyone was away from the home buying items for the funeral, I remember not being able to stay in the house with it being so quiet and I went on a bike ride. I rode quite a distance that day. I remember the breeze, and I remember through all my agony and pain feeling a brief sense of calm. That bike ride helped me put a lot of things in perspective. I'm doing a lot of the things I'm doing today because that single bike ride allowed me the time and space to reformulate and diagnose my new reality.

Find a hobby

I spent this whole book talking about purpose, plan, passion, and persistence. Now I'm going to talk about peace. Without peace it will be almost impossible to find a sense of accomplishment when your purpose comes to realization. Back when I was a teenager, I went to the movies to watch the remake of Brewster's Millions starring Richard Pryor and John Candy. The movie was about a down-on-his-luck minor league baseball player who happens to have an unknown rich uncle who passed away and left Pryor's character his entire inheritance. However, the rich uncle was not impressed with Richard Pryor's character's life and was uncomfortable leaving him with the entire inheritance, so he decided to play a game with Pryor's character. The game was if he is able to spend $30 million in 30 days he would get the entire inheritance of $300 million, but if there was anything left of the initial $30 million, Richard Pryor's character would get nothing.

Towards the end of the 30 days, Richard Pryor's character hated the site of money. He never got to enjoy those 30 days. He eventually won the game and inherited $300 million, but he had a very valuable lesson learned in balancing wealth and sensibility. Richard Pryor's disdain towards achieving his purpose can happen to us if we focus on day in and day out are the steps for achieving that purpose. It is important that you have break times and outlets to take your mind away from the hectic ins and outs of everyday life and your drive toward success. Though there are several dangerous vices that many go to, I would like to use this chapter to steer you toward positive outlets.

One of the great outlets you can have is to find a hobby. This hobby should be something that is not truly related to any of the tasks that you have to achieve your goal. For example, if you are an auto mechanic, it may not be a great hobby to work on cars in your spare time. Though you may love working on cars, doing that to get away from the task of working on cars is counterproductive. However, it may be nice for change to take up painting or something that will get your mind off your work yet allow you to do what you love which is working with your hands.

One thing that I do, if you don't already know, is I play adult league hockey. Currently, I play in two leagues one is ice hockey, and the other is in-line hockey a sport that I recently picked up and quickly grew to love. One thing I love about this outlet is while I am on the rink, I am a hockey player, all the other hats that I wear are literally locked up in the locker room. For one to two hours, I step away from the realities of life and I get to live my childhood dream. Also, it is almost an unwritten rule to not talk about real-life *"stuff"* while sitting on the hockey bench. This is a perfect way to get away and recharge your mind.

Retreat and step back

Franklin Delano Roosevelt was one of the most influential presidents of the 20th century. He presided over the United States during a difficult time of economic depression and world war. In addition, Roosevelt suffered several health problems. Whenever he was feeling worn down, he would go to his personal retreat of Warm Springs, Georgia. This is the place that he loved the most and he would go there to recharge and step back in order to rethink his circumstance and the circumstances of the nation. This retreat helped him in navigating some of the most difficult situations this nation has ever faced. Though I never found a *"place"* to scream as Pastor Meade suggested, I do have a place to go to recharge. As a matter fact, I have two places where I recharge. One such place is Charleston South Carolina, and the other is the Niagara Peninsula of Southern Ontario. Like Roosevelt, I go to those places to reset my perspective and recharge. That is my retreat. If you already do not have a place to retreat, it is imperative that you find one. A retreat can help in clearing your head and stepping away from the hustle and bustle of an issue in view that issue and an outside light.

I have worked with several companies that when it comes time to start their strategic planning phases, the decision-makers and department heads will go away for retreat in order to gain a fresh perspective of their mission, their industry, and their future. When planning for your future, it is important for you to do the same. Being away from the moment is helpful in making sound decisions in determining your purpose and planning for it.

Take breaks

During summers at my grandparents in Brazil Indiana, I remember cutting grass with my grandfather. My grandfather had a great deal of lawn that he had to cut, and he owned three push mowers. My grandfather, my brother, and I would each be given a section of the lawn and we would start to cut. Usually, it was a two-hour process with the three of us cutting. As a young man, I would want to get the grass cut as soon as possible. However, like clockwork, grandfather would come to my section of the lawn, tell me to cut off my lawnmower they could break. The break would usually be about 10 minutes where he would have us get water, use the latrine, (grandfather was career Air Force), and sit down for a minute. After the 10-minute break, we would get up and finish the job. When I was a kid, I really did not like that break because I figured I wasn't tired. However, as I got older, I realized how important it is to take breaks.

In sports breaks are essential. In football, there is halftime after two 15-minute quarters of play. In basketball, there is halftime after the teams have played two 12-minute quarters. Hockey has two intermissions that fit between three 20-minute periods. These breaks in sports are designed for the players to rest and for the coaches and the team to make necessary adjustments due to the way the game is being played. It is essential that this practice is carried over in the non-sports world. Professional and personal breaks are necessary even during the proverbial *"game"* to rest and make adjustments to better adapt to the situation.

I worked in Columbus Indiana at the community college, I would go every Tuesday and Thursday to play lunchtime hockey. This was a great hour-long break in order to free my mind and approach the rest of my day with a clear head. There are many people I know who go to the gym or take a run during their lunch break at work. Though it may not sound like rest, it is indeed a mental break that is necessary to complete the day.

It is important that breaks are implemented in your day. Also, it is imperative that you take at least one day to rest. This day should be used to recover from all the *"hustle and bustle"* that you faced during the week and to be well rested to face all of the *"hustle and bustle"* you will encounter very, very near future. For rest leads to the final P, and that is peace.

Chapter 17

The Power of Trying Something New

In the previous chapter, I emphasized the importance of finding a hobby. While having a consistent interest or activity is key to emotional and mental wellness, there are times when switching things up and trying something new can be just as vital. It keeps the mind active, the spirit curious, and the body invigorated. Embracing new experiences—even when they're out of your comfort zone—can rejuvenate your sense of purpose and help you rediscover joy.

Take, for instance, my experience with roller hockey. I've played ice hockey most of my life, so skating and stickhandling aren't new to me. Yet despite the fact that my father owned a roller skating rink when I was a child, I never once played roller hockey growing up. It wasn't until I moved to Asheville, North Carolina, and discovered there was no ice rink, that I considered roller hockey as an alternative. My only option for ice hockey was to drive to Greenville, South Carolina—until a chance encounter at Carrier Park led me to a roller hockey rink.

What followed was a humbling but fulfilling journey. At 51 years old, I found myself starting over, watching YouTube tutorials, practicing basic drills, and consulting with experienced roller hockey players just to get a grip on the sport. I was clumsy. I was slow. But I was committed. The excitement I felt reminded me of my early days learning ice hockey. Even more importantly, I met new friends, joined a new community, and rediscovered the beginner's joy of simply trying something unfamiliar.

Then came Jo Jackson. If you've read earlier chapters, you know Jo tricked me into joining CrossFit. I say that with love, of course, because at 54 years old, I found myself taking on a sport designed to punish you into fitness. CrossFit is no joke. There's even a machine called the Assault Bike—and trust me, it earns its name. Despite the intimidation factor, I'm now having more fun and seeing more results than I ever thought possible. I'm in the best shape of my life, and I start each morning with purpose, energy, and laughter.

Trying something new isn't just about picking up a hobby—it's about refreshing your mind, body, and spirit. First, it challenges your brain. You're required to think differently, practice problem-solving, and stretch your mental boundaries. Second, it reinvigorates your body by pushing you to move in new ways. And third, it invites new people into your life. Since beginning both roller hockey and CrossFit, I've made lasting connections in the Asheville community and even across the globe—my CrossFit competition team is made up entirely of Australians.

THE 4P'S OF YOU

Stagnation is a hidden enemy. Whether or not we enjoy our daily routines, they often prevent us from seeing what else is possible. Even small changes—like choosing a new vacation destination—can have a powerful impact. So many people fall into the trap of annual repetition: the same beach trip, the same resort, the same restaurants. But what if next year you went somewhere totally new? What if you explored a part of the world you've only seen on TV? You may find beauty, culture, and joy in places you never expected.

Trying something new pulls you out of the mundane and places you into the realm of discovery. It brings peace, sharpens your focus, and renews your sense of self. It can reignite dormant passions or spark entirely new ones. Right now, for instance, I'm learning about Australian Rules Football. I've been binge-watching the Sydney Swans' YouTube channel, and a new friend from Australia who once played the sport has offered to teach me. It's wild to think that my next athletic endeavor could be in a sport I didn't grow up with.

The overarching point is simple: growth doesn't stop when you reach adulthood. It doesn't stop in your 40s, 50s, or 60s. It continues as long as you're willing to stretch. Whether it's learning a new skill, traveling somewhere unfamiliar, or joining a new social circle, trying something new is one of the most rewarding ways to keep your life full of meaning, movement, and magic.

www.ingramcontent.com/pod-product-compliance
Lightning Source LLC
Chambersburg PA
CBHW050905160426
43194CB00011B/2291